OUT OF DARKNESS
INTO HIS MARVELOUS LIGHT

NANCY N. GORE

CREATION HOUSE
A STRANG COMPANY

OUT OF DARKNESS by Nancy N. Gore
Published by Creation House
A Strang Company
600 Rinehart Road
Lake Mary, Florida 32746
www.creationhouse.com

This book or parts thereof may not be reproduced in any form, stored in a retrieval system, or transmitted in any form by any means—electronic, mechanical, photocopy, recording, or otherwise—without prior written permission of the publisher, except as provided by United States of America copyright law.

Unless otherwise noted, all Scripture quotations are from the Holy Bible, New International Version of the Bible. Copyright © 1973, 1978, 1984, International Bible Society. Used by permission.

Scripture quotations marked NAS are from the New American Standard Bible–Updated Edition, Copyright © 1960, 1962, 1963, 1968, 1971, 1972, 1973, 1975, 1977, 1995 by The Lockman Foundation. Used by permission. (www.Lockman.org)

Scripture quotations marked NKJV are from the New King James Version of the Bible. Copyright © 1979, 1980, 1982 by Thomas Nelson, Inc., publishers. Used by permission.

Scripture quotations marked KJV are from the King James Version of the Bible.

Scripture quotations marked ASV are from the American Standard Bible. Copyright © 1960, 1962, 1968, 1971, 1972, 1973, 1975, by the Lockman Foundation. Used by permission.

Design Director: Bill Johnson
Cover designer: Amanda Potter

Copyright © 2008 by Nancy N. Gore
All rights reserved

Library of Congress Control Number: 2008932493
International Standard Book Number: 978-1-59979-457-0

First Edition

08 09 10 11 12 — 987654321
Printed in the United States of America

DEDICATION

I would like to dedicate this book to my late husband, Carson "Harry" Gore, who was loving and supportive in so many ways. He encouraged me to stretch my boundaries.

TABLE OF CONTENTS

Introduction 1

one
Mercy, Grace, and Love 3

two
Seek My Face 17

three
In His Presence 29

four
Bought with a Price 39

five
Called Out of Darkness 47

six
Trust and Obey 57

seven
Possess the Land 69

eight
You Are My Witness 81

INTRODUCTION

I HAVE WRITTEN THIS book in obedience to the Lord. It was not my desire to open myself up to vulnerability and criticism by sharing my weaknesses and trials with the world. These are words given to me by the Holy Spirit in times of desperation, hurt, anger, and pain. Jesus said in John 10, "His sheep follow Him because they know His voice. But they will never follow a stranger...because they do not recognize a stranger's voice" (vv. 4–5). It has been my prayer when seeking the Lord and waiting before Him that I would hear and know His voice and no other.

I began seeking to hear God out of desperation more than anything. I had been through several years of depression and deep hurt and had sought comfort in worldly ways rather than in God. "After all," I thought, "He had allowed the circumstances hadn't He? Could I really trust Him?" Deep down I knew the answer and was desperately trying to find my way back to Him.

Thus came the words of comfort and the promise of light ahead. It was not an easy journey. The cloud of darkness was so heavy at times, and I would seek comfort in the familiar, earthly ways. Through it all, though, God showed me His grace and mercy. His light was waiting at the end of the tunnel. The Lord has instructed me to share these words with others who are struggling to find their way out of the darkness and into His marvelous light.

We cannot comprehend the love that He has for us. Indeed, we cannot comprehend the Cross and the price He willingly paid there for us. He, God's own Son, suffered separation from God the Father to bear our sins. He made the gift of grace so easy that we stumble over it! We try to add works to it. We try to earn it, but it is a complete and finished work. He is waiting for you with outstretched arms.

The story of the prodigal son is a perfect picture of God's forgiveness, grace, and love. I thank Him every day, for I could not have made it through without Him.

one
MERCY, GRACE, AND LOVE

Storms in the Desert

I AM THE BEGINNING and the end, the Alpha and Omega, the first and the last! All things are through Me. You must trust Me in the things that I allow in your life. They will help you to grow, just as storms in the desert cause growth from the parched earth. They will never be more than you can handle, and I will be with you always. I never leave you. Sometimes you forget that I am there, but I never leave. Don't you know that I love you? I only allow the things that will help you to grow.

Come, dine with Me, feast at My table; be strengthened, that you might grow!

You Are My Tools

> For as high as the heavens are above the earth, so great
> is his love for those who *fear* him.
> —PSALM 103:11, EMPHASIS ADDED

My child, you have not understood what it means to fear Me.

It bothers you. It is not a trembling fear, for you cannot love someone you are afraid of. This kind of fear is not from Me.

You must love Me, for perfect love casts out fear.[1] This word means to have an overwhelming awe of My great power.

I do not use My power as men would, to threaten or cajole into obedience. Indeed, I have used it to redeem you from the consequences of your sin. I want your loving service, not fearful obedience. Indeed, My loving-kindness is great toward you. You cannot possibly understand how great it is. Just accept it in the love with which it is given. My love is great toward you.

You are My joy and hope. You are also My arms and My legs. You are My tools to share the gospel.

Many have not heard, and few understand after hearing. They are deceived by their own intellect and the lies of the world (Satan). You must pray for their understanding, and you must share the truth with them—My truth, not the world's.

For I am the way, the only way. Listen and obey My instruction.

My Grace Is Sufficient

Come, eat with Me, drink with Me, sit at My table, and feast on My riches, for you are My child and I love you! Do not be concerned about your weaknesses. I will not put you in a place for which I have not prepared you. My love is not dependant on you or how much you grow.

I love you just as you are, *without* your works. Works are a part of the Law, and they are dead.

My grace is sufficient to cover every weakness you have, even those you never overcome. Don't you see? I paid the price for you. I have redeemed you. Walk in My redemption and My love. Rest in Me, and let Me do the rest.

---

[1] 1 John 4:8

You Are Unique (for M. G.)

I have called you to come apart and be separate from the world. I have a work for you to do. It is your work. No one else can do it as you can, for you are unique. You know that I have called you; but you have been afraid to trust Me with your every need, and your needs have been great. Tell Me—has the world met your needs? Has all your worry and running to and fro provided the security that you desire?

I have sent you a gift this day. I tell you it is only a small drop in the bucket of what I will supply if you will but trust Me, for I love you with a great love. You must learn to trust Me and look to Me for all of your needs. You think that I have let you down in the past, but you never really let go to let Me work My perfect will in these things. I am able, even now, to take all of your mistakes and use them for good. I am able to meet all of your needs if you will but trust Me. I have called you out from the world. I have set you apart for My service. I have chosen you and called you by name.

You have labored long in the world. Come to Me, and I will give you rest.

The world has not met your needs. I have sent good and perfect gifts from above and met your needs even when your faith was lacking. Think what I can do when your faith is strong!

I have waited long for you, My child. I am still waiting.

I love you, and would that you be strong in your faith. That means that you must trust Me, even if you don't see the answer. Sight is not faith, but faith will bring it to pass.

I long for your love and your fellowship. Come and dine with Me. Feast at My table, and I will teach you many truths and show you many things, great and mighty things that you know not![2]

---

2 Jeremiah 33:3

Spread Your Wings

> For it is by grace you have been saved, through faith—and this not from yourselves, it is the gift of God—not by works, so that no one can boast.
> —Ephesians 2:8–9

Grace is not a small thing, My child. It is greater than you can imagine.

You are My child, and My grace is sufficient to carry you through every trial and every circumstance. My grace saw Jesus through His darkest hour, when the weight of the world's sin was on His shoulders. My grace will see your loved one through his hour of need. It is in this time that he will reach out to Me, and I will be there. I will not leave him or forsake him. My love is great toward him. I long to comfort him. I long to put My arms about him. But he must let Me.

My Word says:

> You have not because you ask not.
> —Matthew 7:7

> Ask, and you will receive, so that your joy may be made full.
> —John 16:24, NAS

I do not impose on your free will. I long to give you many things, but you do not ask. I long to set you free, but you do not see your own bondage.

Know the truth, and it will set you free. Know My Word and the promises that are yours. Cultivate faith in My Word. As you see new truths, your faith will grow. Then, you will surely "call to Me, and I will answer you, and show you great and mighty things, which you do not know" (Jer. 33:3, NKJV). I am here waiting for you to call upon Me and test your faith.

Spread your wings and learn to soar. Each time you try your wings, they get stronger and surer. Your faith will grow and be stronger each time you see your faith turn into action and your prayers answered. Remember: you have not because you ask not. What do you have to lose by asking? I am here waiting.

All Things New

Oh, My child, I love you so.

Don't you see? It is not your righteousness that enables you to come to Me. It is My blood and My righteousness. I have set you free! You do not have to walk in darkness. You do not have to deserve forgiveness; you have but to ask. Set your heart toward Me and do not look back.

Do not recall the former things, for, behold, I do a new thing![3] Watch Me, trust Me, cultivate faithfulness in My Word. I see your weaknesses. I also see your desire to please Me. I can work all things together for good; even your weaknesses.

You are My child and I will never let you go. No one shall pluck you out of My hand.[4]

Call unto Me, My child, and I will answer you. Pour out your heart before Me. I know already what is in it.

I am able to save to the uttermost parts of the earth. I am able to make all things new. I am able to part the waters and to make a way in the desert.

Will you not trust Me? Trust and faith come before action. Cultivate faith in Me and in My Word. I will not leave you, nor will I forsake you, even in your darkest hour.[5] Even in your rebellion I was with you, and I understood why you were feeling the way you were. I created you and all of your emotions.

I remember your beginnings, how you came from dust.

---

3 Isaiah 43:19
4 John 10:29, KJV
5 Joshua 1:5

I call to your remembrance My faithfulness in the past. I am God; is anything to difficult for Me?[6]

I am your God, your Father in heaven. Come and fellowship with Me. Bring Me your joys and your sorrow. I can handle both, and I can turn your sorrows into joy! Lean on Me and not on others, for man will fail you. He is not perfect or holy, as I am perfect and holy.

I am here for you—waiting—always!

Grieving the Holy Spirit

> And do not grieve the Holy Spirit of God, with whom you were sealed for the day of redemption.
> —Ephesians 4:30

My child, I love you and I long to fellowship with you.

I am here waiting, always. Why do you delay in coming to Me? It matters not how you come to Me. If your heart is not cleansed, I will cleanse it. If your mind is not quiet, I will still it. Do not let the enemy rob you of fellowship with these lies—and they are lies! Nothing can stand between you and My love for you. I long to fellowship with you just as you are.

You grieve the Holy Spirit by quenching Him. You quench Him in many ways:

- by not hearing when He speaks to you
- by not trusting in My promises
- by not coming aside when I call

I call and you hear not. I speak and you obey not.

I am worthy of your trust and your praise. I am not man, that I should fail you. I am God, Elohim, the great and mighty I AM who is perfect and holy in every way! My love for you is

---

[6] Jeremiah 32:27, NAS

perfect, lacking in nothing. So why do you not trust Me? You ask, how am I not trusting You? By taking things into your own hands! By not backing off and letting Me do My work. By lacking in self-control in many areas of your life. I cannot work with you in My way. I have ordained that things be accomplished, but until you release them to Me, I cannot work! Jobs, circumstances, relationships—loose them all to Me. Back off; it is a choice of your will. I will help you, My daughter, but you must let Me help you. Surrender your will to Me. Let go and trust Me. I will not fail you. I love your more than any man could ever love you.

I have redeemed you; you belong to Me. I am a jealous God.

Seek ye first the kingdom of God, and *then* all other things shall be given you.[7]

His Strength; My Weakness

> My grace is sufficient for you, for my power is made perfect in weakness.
> —2 Corinthians 12:9

I love you, My child, with a love that is greater than any man's love. I long for your fellowship. I am pleased when you bring your troubles to Me, no matter how worldly they may be. I am able to teach you many truths through these trials. Look to Me for the answers. My ways are not man's way. I would that you would see the great love that I have for you. Man's love is imperfect and will fail you in many ways.

My love is perfect even as I am perfect. I will never leave you nor forsake you.[8] I will be your strong and mighty right hand. I will be strong in your behalf. I will help you to let go, My child, and to trust Me. It will not be easy, for these roots have been

---

7 Matthew 6:33
8 Hebrews 13:5

growing for many years and are rooted deep in your soul. It will take a daily dying out to self. You must learn to walk in My Spirit. When you learn to sense My presence with you and walk in My presence, you will not feel lonely or afraid.

You come into My presence, but you do not stay there. Learn to take Me with you in all that you do. Commune with Me in all that you do.

Fellowship with Me through My Word, and I will teach you many things. I am in all things. Trust Me and praise Me in every situation. Then watch Me work, and do not try to help Me. You only get in My way and slow Me down! Praise and trust go hand in hand. Use them to loose My perfect will in every situation.

Cultivating Faith

> O Lord, when you favored me, you made my mountain to stand firm.
> —Psalm 30:7

My child, hear My voice and listen to Me, and I will show you many truths.

I have come to you today, because you have asked. I love you, and I am here waiting for you always! My love for you is sufficient; it will fill all of your needs as you bring them to Me. Bring Me your husband, your children, all of your loved ones. I am able to bring them back, but it must be in My time.

Sometimes, I do allow mountains to stand in your life (and theirs). Without them, you would not seek Me.

Worldly things and fleshly things cannot fill your needs. There are voids in your life that only I can fill. The world is like a maze with many dead-end paths. It takes a listening ear and an obedient heart to stay on the right path. It is so easy to be drawn aside. The enemy is so subtle at times that much discernment is needed. Train your ear to know My voice and pray for discernment. Test the spirits and see if they are of Me. Know My Word, for My Word is truth.[9] It never varies.

There is no shadow of turning with Me. There is no variation in My love for you. Whether you are obedient or disobedient, I love you the same.

However, I cannot fulfill your needs if you will not trust Me! Perfect love casts out fear.[10] Know that My love for you is perfect in every way. Trust Me. I have brought you a great distance. Soon you will look back and see how far you have come. I open many doors for you. It will take trust and faith to walk through them. Keep your eyes on Me and cultivate faith in Me and in My Word. My Word is truth, and truth will set you free. Be free, My child, from every bondage. I set you free this day, My child, for I have seen your willing heart. Set your face like a flint, and do not turn back![11]

I will give you strength, My child, in the moment that you need it. I am your strength and your fortress. Run to Me when your own strength fails.

I am here for you always, no matter what. My love toward you is great. My love is strong toward you and will strengthen you in your weakness. My love is freedom and not bondage.

A Love Letter

> Lead me, O LORD, in your righteousness because of my enemies—make straight your way before me.
> —PSALM 5:8

My child, I have called you to a work. I am preparing you so that you will be equipped for the task ahead. Yes, I go ahead of

---

9 John 17:17
10 1 John 4:18
11 Isaiah 50:7

you and prepare the way. I put up fences when necessary to keep your way straight. The enemy would distract you in many ways and has thrown many obstacles in your path. He has slowed your progress, but he will not stop you. You have only to look up and keep your eyes on Me, for I am the light that illumines your path. There is no darkness in Me.

When darkness comes, you must not fear. Remember: the light that is within you is greater that the darkness. With a word from you, the darkness must vanish, for I have given you authority over all the powers of darkness. The darkness that you have allowed in, called depression, is also subject to the authority that I have given you.

There will be trials and tribulations in the flesh. There will be deaths of loved ones that you will not understand.

You must cultivate faith and trust in Me if you are to keep your head above the circumstances. You cannot see the whole picture, nor will you understand some things in this lifetime. You must trust in Me and in My Word. Know My Word, for it is truth. Know the truth and you will be set free. To trust Me you must develop an intimate relationship with Me. Come away from the world and all of its cares and spend time with Me. I am always here waiting for you. I desire, even long, for your fellowship. I will teach you many things, if you will but let Me.

When I see you hurting and floundering when the darkness and despondency comes, I hurt with you! I long to wrap My arms around you. Why do you wait so long to come to Me when you know I am there waiting for you? The enemy speaks lies of condemnation and unworthiness to keep you from coming. Why do you listen to him? It is My voice you should be listening to.

You must train your ear to hear My voice. Come aside and listen, for I am here, always, waiting on you. I love you with a great love.[12] You have been through much. I have tested you and tried you. Your flesh has been weak and failed you many times. In your heart there has always been a desire to please Me and do what is right. I have seen your struggle. It has been a long one, and it has been great. This, too, shall pass. The season of testing is coming to a close.

I am calling you to a new walk, a different walk. It is so important to cultivate a listening ear and to know My voice! Hear Me when I call; come quickly and do not delay. I will meet with you and show you many things—"great and mighty things, which you do not know" (Jer. 33:3, NKJV). This will take discipline of the flesh, but I will help you. I will help you in all things; you have only to ask Me. I am here waiting, but I will not interfere with your free will.

I call, but you must come. I speak, but you must listen. I give, but you must receive.

Will you not receive the great love and the gifts that I have for you? I have spread a table of many fine delicacies. I have engraved the invitation in wood and signed it in My blood. I have sent it on the wings of My messengers and laid it at your feet. It is stained with the tears of My grieving, for I wait, but you do not come. I call, but you do not answer. I speak, but you do not hear.

Is it any wonder that the light is hidden, so you cannot find your way? I speak not to condemn you, but to call you. You long for your children to come and fellowship with you, but they are too busy. I long for your fellowship, for you are My child. I love you with an eternal love that can never be diminished. Thank you for coming today, My child. Please remember: I am always here for you. *I love you.*

---

12   Ephesians 2:4

When You Are Hurt

My child, I will come to you, even in the midst of trouble and heartache. I am here always waiting for you, but when you are hurting it is harder for you to hear My voice.

There will always be hurts and disappointments in life. You must learn to give them to Me quickly so they will not eat at you or your faith. Some hurts are for your own good. You ask, how are they for my good? I will tell you. You must learn that your happiness does not depend on any man (or person). Only I can bring you happiness and peace of mind. When you look to people, they will fail you, even as you have failed others. They are imperfect, even as you are imperfect.

My love is the only perfect love. Perfect love casts out fear.

Why do you fear the future? Do you not know that I care about your happiness and your smallest needs? I see the desires of your heart. I will work things out for you, but only if you trust Me. I am not limited by earthly means. You cannot figure out My ways, so do not even try. Only trust Me to work for your good in every situation and every area of your life. This requires loosing every situation and every relationship to Me. It will not be easy.

It will be a daily walk of trust and obedience. Obedience requires trust. Trust requires love. You must know My perfect love for you, so come daily and let Me share My love with you. I long for your presence at My feet. I long to hold you and share your hurts and remove the burden of those hurts. Come just as you are, with every imperfection, every hurt, every need. I long to share them as your closest friend would and offer comfort.

Pour out your heart to Me. I will understand, and I will not criticize.

MY GRACE AND MY LOVE!

My child, you need not fear coming into My presence. I do not condemn you when you delay coming. My love is not human; it is not conditional or imperfect. You delay coming to Me and even fear or dread it at times because you feel you haven't measured up. I don't have a yardstick, My child. You do not have to measure up.

Christ redeemed you from the Law, with its curse and fear of punishment![13] You are under the cover of My grace and My love. I would set you free from the fear of rejection and punishment.

My love is not conditional. My arms are always open.

My love is perfect, and perfect love casts out fear.[14] The time will come when you will not fear. You will understand completely My perfect love, and you will share it with others.

I go with you today, My child, and I order your steps. Know that I am with you even if you mess up. I am teaching you and strengthening you in all areas of your life—yes, even in the self-discipline. You are making progress, My child, even if you don't see it. Remember I am here, My child. I am always here!

---

13 Galatians 3:13
14 1 John 4:18

two
SEEK MY FACE

Come and Dine

This is how you can recognize the Spirit of God: Every spirit that acknowledges that Jesus Christ has come in the flesh is from God.

—1 John 4:2

My child, I confess that Jesus Christ came in the flesh and dwelt among men. I am the Living Word, and I speak to you through My Holy Spirit. I come to fellowship with you, for you are My child.

I long to teach you many truths, but you must learn to be still before Me. As you do this, your ear becomes more tuned to hear My Spirit speaking to you. You have seen this already, but you have only begun. Come, dine with Me daily, My child, for you must eat often to grow spiritually as well as physically. When the cells of your body have no nourishment, they cannot function properly. This is true of your spirit man also. Feed him daily through My Word and through fellowship with Me, for I am the Living Word. I have set the table in abundance for you. I have much to teach you and to show you. I am here waiting for you as often as you will come. Go today with your ear tuned to hear My voice.

Cultivate a Listening Ear

> His sheep follow Him because they know His voice. But they will never follow a stranger...because they do not recognize a stranger's voice.
>
> —John 10:4-5

Cultivate a listening ear, My child, so that you may be able to hear My voice when I speak to you. Sheep recognize their master's voice quickly because it is a familiar voice, one they hear constantly. Come before Me often with a listening ear. My voice will become a familiar one, one you will recognize quickly. I long to fellowship with you, just as you long to fellowship with your children. You are hurt when they prefer others' company to yours. I am grieved when you do not seek My fellowship.

Don't you know that I understand everything you are going through, your doubts, your fears? I do not condemn you for them, but I help you to overcome them! I long to be your comforter.

I long to be your teacher also. I have many things to share with you, if you will but come aside with a listening ear and let Me. I come to you in the still of the night. Your ear must be tuned to hear My voice. Soon you will know My voice and will recognize quickly when a stranger speaks to you. Soon you will hear Me quickly day or night, even when you are busy, but only if you cultivate a listening ear so that My voice is a very familiar one to your ear.

Seek Me daily and seek Me early. I will order your day for you and redeem the time when you seek Me first.

In quietness and in rest before Me will you find strength. When you become weary, lay down your load at My feet and cast all your cares on Me. I will give you peace and rest for your soul. My yoke is easy and My burden is light.[15] Walk in the grace and in the freedom I have given you. Clothe yourself with the garment of praise, for I am your source! Keep your eyes on Me and not on circumstances.

I AM ABLE!

My child, I am pleased that you have come before Me with your praise and thanksgiving. I have seen your heart and your desire to please Me. It matters not that you sometimes miss Me in your decisions. I am able to work all things for good, yes, and even to correct your errors. My ways are not your ways, nor My timetable yours.[16] Trust and faith are the keys that unlock the doors to My promises.

Do not doubt My Word, even if you don't see any answers. My Word will not return to Me void. It accomplishes what I have sent it forth to accomplish![17]

My Word is truth and not a lie. Every promise that I have given you is yours. I do not repent of My promises or take them back. They require only your faith to see them accomplished. Your faith is great in many areas but weak in some. My written and spoken Word will strengthen your faith. Seek Me and seek My Word for strength in your life.

I am always here for you, always waiting, always listening. Seek My guidance daily, and I will help you to stay on the right paths. If you stray, I will help you find your way back. I do not condemn you for your errors. I do not condemn you for your fleshly nature, but I do help you to overcome it if you will let Me.

---

15   Matthew 11:30
16   Isaiah 55:8
17   Isaiah 55:11

I Confess My Weakness (My Prayer)

Lord, I feel so empty and so alone, and I know I should not, for You are with me. You have never left or forsaken me. It is I who lost sight of You and Your love for me.

I have sought fulfillment elsewhere, and even though fleeting, it is satisfying for the moment. Please forgive me for my weakness. I confess my weakness to You, for I have tried everything I know to overcome it. I cannot. So I come to You just as I am and say, Lord I cannot do it! Please Lord, can You do it for me? Your Word tells me that Your strength is made perfect in my weakness.[18] It will have to be Your strength, Lord, for I have none of my own.

Lord, I need to feel Your presence with me. I need the emptiness filled. I cast this care upon You and ask You to replace it with that peace that passes all understanding.

The Refining Process

My child, come to Me, for I am waiting. I hear your voice calling to Me, and I will answer. You are Mine, bought with a price. Great was that price and great will be your deliverance—and your family's, yes, even your children and loved ones you have believed for. They will come, for I have called them! They are Mine, for I speak things that are not as though they were.[19] This is faith, My child, to call things that are not as though the were.

There is no present and future with Me, for I know the outcome already. Yes, and I know your outcome, My child, for I

---

18 1 Corinthians 12:9, KJV
19 Romans 4:17

have called you to a work and I am preparing you. The refining process is never easy; it is even harder when you fight Me or resist. It is so much easier to submit to what I am teaching you. Praise Me in the midst of every circumstance and keep your eyes on Me, for I am your source of strength and deliverance. I am your source, My child; besides Me there is no other!

Look not to man to meet your needs or give you answers. Seek Me first and seek Me often, for I will be your teacher. I will use others to teach you also, but I would have you seek Me first. I long for your trust in every situation. I have many things to show you, and I long, yes, even hunger for your fellowship.

Perfect Love

My daughter, I am pleased that you have sought Me this morning. I see your weariness and your heaviness of mind, and it is difficult for you to feel as if you can receive a word from Me in this frame of mind. But it is your spirit that I commune with and not your mind. You have been obedient, and even now the heaviness is lifting, for I desire to fellowship with you and would have your mind clear to hear My voice. I love you with a great love, and My hand is upon you in everything you do.

Keep your ear tuned to My voice, and I will lead you throughout the day. If you stray to the right or to the left, I will draw you back to My path and My ways, for you are My child. You seek answers to many questions. They will come, but not all at once. You are not ready for all the answers. You still have drawings of the flesh, and you fear slipping again. But do not fear, My daughter, for if you do slip, I will be there to catch you. You will not fall headlong. I know your weaknesses, and I use them to teach you and, yes, even to strengthen you! You are Mine, and I have called you. I have many gifts for you, and I will use you mightily. Yes, I said mightily. Do not be concerned how or even when. Each day has enough cares of its own.[20] Come to Me daily to seek Me early, and I will direct your steps.

Oh, My child, if only you knew how much I love you. If only you could comprehend My love for you, you would never fear again, for truly perfect love casts out fear, as recorded in 1 John. John knew My perfect love, and it set him free even while in captivity. My love is upon you, and I will never forsake you, no matter what! Receive My love freely, My child, for freely I give it. Go, and I go with you. Seek Me in all that you do.

ONE WAY

Come quickly, My child, for I have many things to share with you.

I am your God, and I am in the midst of thee. Seek Me with your whole heart and you will find Me. Many do not seek with their whole heart, and this is why they are led astray. There are many false doctrines that teach worldly ways, but My ways are not of the world. My way is truth.

The only way of salvation is through the shed blood of My Son, Jesus Christ! He died for your sins, that you might stand holy and pure before Me. I have made it so easy, but man tries to make it so hard.

You can't be good enough; you can't earn it through the Law, for it is impossible to keep. Don't you think I would have spared My Son if there were any other way? Don't be deceived by doctrines that add to or take away from My Word. My Word is truth. Know the truth, and the truth shall set you free.[21] If you know My Word, you cannot be deceived. I will not tell you anything that contradicts My written Word.

---

20 Matthew 6:34
21 John 8:32

Seek Me with your whole heart and you shall find Me. The enemy is very subtle, at times, to slip lies into the truth. You must be alert. Satan used Scripture to try to tempt Jesus. He will use the Word to deceive you if you let him. You must study My Word and pray for discernment in every area of your life.

Your friend is very precious to Me, and I desire to fellowship with her. I see her hurts and disappointments, and I long to put My arms around her and comfort her through My Holy Spirit. But she must trust Me with her whole heart. She has fears and reservations that hold her back, but she can trust Me, for I desire only her happiness and peace of mind.

There will be trials and storms in every life, but I am able to give you peace in the midst of the storm. All that is required is your trust. Know that I am able to bring good out of every circumstance in your life. Will you not trust Me and, yes, even praise Me for everything in your life?

Faith is the key that unlocks the storehouse of all of My promises. My Word brings and builds faith in you, My child, and I long for your trust in every area of your life.

I am pleased that you have sought Me today, My child. I order your steps for you when you seek Me early. I shelter you from worry and fear when your heart is stayed on Me. Do not receive fear today, My child, for fear is not from Me. Keep your eyes on Me and not on circumstances. Know that I am in control, and I am able to change circumstances in the blink of an eye! All I require is your trust.

Flesh vs. Spirit

My child, come into fellowship with Me this morning, for I desire to teach you many things. My hand is upon you. Do not be amazed at the changes you see in yourself and in others around you, for I am working in and through you. I am working to purify your motives in every area of your life.

I trust you with My gifts and My calling.
I trust you to let Me accomplish that which concerns you.
You are not able to make the changes you desire. It cannot be done in the flesh, for flesh cannot overcome flesh. It must be done in the spirit and by My Spirit, saith the Lord. I have overcome all obstacles through My blood. I make you an overcomer, also.

I Will Satisfy

My child, come to Me and sup with Me, and I will show you many things. I will fill you and satisfy all your hunger and emptiness.

Stay in My presence and walk in My presence, and you will never be lonely again. I am your source and the only one that can fill the emptiness. No man can meet all your needs. No friend can fully understand like I can. I see into the heart; they cannot!

I see your hurts, angers, and disappointments. I understand your desires even when they are fleshly. I am also able to take away the hurts and anger and change the desires, but first you must submit them to Me. I do not move against your will, but I can use circumstances to show you the need for you to let them go. These feelings only rob you of your peace and joy. I would that you have peace and joy in every situation. This only comes from trust in Me and submission in all areas of your life.

Out of Darkness

I meet with you here today, for you are My child. I have called you, and I have entrusted you to a work. I am indeed preparing you and training you for that work even now. I know there are times you do not see any progress, but there is progress, My child, and you are on My timetable.

I have seen the cries of your heart to be set totally free from the things that so easily beset you: depression, despondency, apathy. I am clearing the path in front of you. No longer will these things continually rise up to entangle you. I have seen your desire to be free. It has not all been your doing or your lack of faith.

There has been a strong battle in the heavenlies to keep your spiritual growth from coming forth, for you will be a strong and mighty warrior for your family, and you will lead others into battle for their families also. Great will be the strength of your prayers in the heavenlies, for you will be a mighty warrior and your weapon will be one of truth. My Word is truth, and it is sharper than any two-edged sword! [22]I have given you this weapon to be victorious.

My daughter, I have called you out of darkness into My light. I will shine the light into every dark corner of your life. Nothing shall be hidden. All the past hurts shall be revealed, so they can never haunt you again! I send forth My Word to heal the hurts. My truth will set you free so that you can go set others free. Do not lose heart; the battle is Mine, saith the Lord, and I will accomplish My purpose in you!

By My Spirit

Not by might, nor by power, but by My Spirit, saith the Lord![23] All things are accomplished through My Spirit, and without My Holy Spirit nothing is accomplished. Nothing can be accomplished in the flesh. Therefore, it is important to seek My will in everything you do. Your obedience is important, and you are learning to act more quickly when I speak. Even a small thing

---
22 Hebrews 4:12, NKJV
23 Zechariah 4:6

may not seem important, but it is a step in teaching complete trust and obedience. I am pleased with your progress. You came aside this morning because I spoke. Timing is so very important. A short delay may not seem like much, but circumstances can change quickly. You are here, and I am pleased.

Your praises were a sweet aroma to Me. They were truly a sacrifice of praise, for you did not feel it but chose to praise Me by faith. You have chosen to walk the faith walk for your husband and your children. You have chosen to trust My Word, even when you don't see any changes.

I watch over My Word to perform it, every written word and every spoken word.[24] They will not return unto Me void.[25] Have I not said it, and will I not do it?

Am I a man that I should lie?[26] I think not! For I am your God, and I move mightily for you, My child. Yes, I said *mightily*! I have stored up riches for you, because you have been faithful. Those who are faithful over small things, I will make ruler over much.[27] You shall have much, My child. You shall lack nothing either spiritually or physically. You shall prosper and be in health, even as your spirit/soul prospers.[28] Spirit and soul shall line up with My Word. My Word is truth, and truth will set you free.[29]

This is not far off, My child, as you may think. You are learning quickly and looking to Me, even when under the blanket of heaviness that besets you. I am faithful and will not leave you comfortless.[30] I go before you and prepare the way for you today, My child.

---

24 Jeremiah 1:12, NAS
25 Isaiah 55:11
26 Numbers 23:19
27 Matthew 25:23, NAS
28 3 John 2
29 John 8:32
30 John 14:18, KJV

I have said, "Seek My face," and you have said, "Thy face I shall seek." You have called, and I have answered. You shall have the peace and the joy that you have sought. This is My promise unto you, My child, for I have seen your faithfulness even when you could not see the light at the end of the tunnel. But the light is coming—and soon, My child, for I am moving on your behalf. I am strong for you and do battle for you in the heavenlies.

For, indeed, you have been sifted like wheat, but the chaff has fallen aside and only the choice grain remains. It will bear much fruit when watered. This too will come.

You say, when? But you must not run ahead of Me. Listen to My voice and follow, even as I have been teaching you. Flow with My Spirit, and I will direct you. Go forth today, My child, and I go with you. I will direct your steps, even as you have asked.

Created for Fellowship

I have been waiting here for you. I am pleased that you have come.

There is still reluctance when I call, and you get sidetracked easily on your way to our meeting place. But you will come to know Me as a friend that sticketh closer than a brother.[31] Then you will come with joy and expectation, and you will look forward to these times together. I long for you to know how much I love you and care about your smallest needs.

I created you to have fellowship with Me, but the father of lies would tell you that I am here to condemn you and that I don't understand your needs. Not understand? I created you with each of those feelings and emotions. You have the ability to feel much sorrow and pain. It gives you the ability to care for

---

31 Proverbs 18:24

others and their needs. It also gives you vulnerability to being hurt and used by others, but I would not have you void of these feelings.

My child, I love you so much, and I do care even about your smallest needs.

I know what it is like to hurt for your children when they are hurting. I know what it is like to long for love and companionship. Was not man created in My image and likeness?[32]

I, too, long for the love and fellowship of My chosen ones. I long for your companionship and love. I will lead you, My child, into that perfect love that casts out fear. You will come to know Me and trust Me through these times together.

I do not condemn you when you get sidetracked. Only know that I am here waiting for you with open arms, always! I love you, My child, and My hand is upon you to accomplish that which concerns you. I have heard your prayers and your heart's cries for your loved ones. I am moving to change things in your household. There will be a shaking to remove the cobwebs and debris. When the dust settles, there will be glory in thy household, for you have called and I have answered. Thus saith the Lord.

---

32 Genesis 1:26

three
IN HIS PRESENCE

Look Not to Man

I AM THE WORD of Life. Trust Me, My daughter, concerning the words that I have given you. Feast on My riches. Yes, dine at My table, feed your soul, even as your spirit is fed, and they will line up together with the Word of God. My Word is truth, and it never varies. I change not. There is no shadow of turning with Me.[33] Come, drink from My cup and be filled. I am all that you need, and I can fill all of your needs.

Look not to man. He is but dust and imperfect in all of his ways. Men will fail you, but I will never leave you nor forsake you.[34]

You have but to trust Me and act on My Word. I will not allow your foot to be moved or to stumble. If you miss Me, I will draw you back and teach you from it. Act out of obedience, and I will honor it. Indeed, I will honor you, little one, and great will be your reward. Your are mine, little one. You were bought with a price, so glorify Me in you. Trust and obey; act on My Word. I will speak to you in the night; be ready to hear. As you seek Me, the hearing will come. The next step is to act. When you do not act on My Word, it is blown away with the wind, and it feeds no one. You must trust and obey to have true

---
33 James 1:17, NKJV
34 Hebrews 13:5, NKJV

fellowship with Me. Every friendship is built on trust. Should Mine be any different?

I want to be your closest friend, the one who will be there when others fail. I want to be the one you seek first above all others. Therefore, you must know that I only want happiness and peace of mind for you. Come and drink from My cup and dine at My table and you will be filled.

New Truths

> And we proclaim to you the eternal life, which was with the Father and has appeared to us.
> —John 1:2

I am eternal life to all who believe. I came that you might have abundant life, free from the encumbrance of this world. I come in fullness to all who will let Me! I long to fellowship with you, to show you new truths from My Word that you have not seen before. Seek ye out of the Book and read. Enlightenment will come to you. You will learn of Me and come to know Me. I will no longer be a stranger to you, an entity. I will be a friend, a brother, and a Father. Whatever your needs are, I long to fill them. I would that you be complete and lacking in nothing.[35] Man cannot fill your innermost needs. You were created to have fellowship with Me.

True Fellowship

You are My child, and you have fellowship with Me. I come to you and sup with you and you draw strength from Me. Come away from the world and seek My presence. I long to fellowship with you.

35　James 1:4

I will lead you and guide you into a new and deeper worship. You will be strengthened in your spirit and in your mind as you dwell in My presence and conform your mind to your spirit and My Spirit! This is true fellowship with Me, and it comes only from dwelling in My presence.

Seek Me early in the day, and you will not miss Me. You will be tuned into My presence throughout the day. Know that I am with you always, even in your darkest moments when you do not feel My presence. These come less often as you learn to fellowship and yield to My Spirit. I bring joy and peace and harmony into your life. Who on Earth can give you these?

Turning Loose

My peace I give to you—not as the world gives.[36] My peace flows from the very throne of God as you lift up your eyes and look to Me. I offer you peace in the midst of a storm.

As you look to Me for all of your needs, know that I am there waiting to take the cares of the world off of your shoulders. You do not have to carry them. They are mine. I died for them. It is so simple; just give them to Me. Reach out your hands and let them go. It is a symbolic act of your will. Trust Me to work all things together for good in every member of your household.

Trust Me with your loved ones. More importantly, trust Me with yourself and your needs. I know them even better than you do. I understand your thoughts and your feelings. They are so very human, and you *are* human, My child! You will have doubts at times, but remember to look to Me, for I am your answer. I do not condemn you for your humanness.

Condemnation is not from Me. Guilt is not from Me.

My sheep hear My voice and know My voice.[37] It is love, for I am love!

---

36 John 14:27
37 John 10:4

I long to hold you in My arms and comfort you. I want to wipe the tears from your eyes, for you are My child; I have begotten you. I have called your name and brought you forth from the moment of conception. My hand is upon you, even now. Know that I am ever with you. I will never leave you nor forsake you.[38] You are mine, no matter where you go or what you do, so receive My peace today and know that I love you.

Avoiding the Darkness

> If we claim to have fellowship with him yet walk in darkness, we lie and do not live by the truth.
> —1 John 1:6

My child, I am the light, and you must fellowship with Me to avoid the darkness. This does not mean to go in your own direction without seeking My will. My will is easy for you to know, if you but seek Me. It is easy to get sidetracked with the cares and worries of each day.

Put on the mantle of praise every morning as you arise. Praise brings your spirit into fellowship with My Spirit.

Your trust and faith in Me frees Me to work in every situation.

I would have you walk in the light. To avoid the darkness, you must keep your eyes on Me. I am your deliverance. I am the knight in shining armor that comes to your rescue. Man will fail to meet your needs, for you were made to have fellowship with Me. Your fellowship with men must be in Me to be fully satisfying. Seek Me early and you will not miss Me.

---

38 Hebrews 13:5.

Take Up My Gifts

I am pleased that you are seeking Me and desire to hear My voice. I come to you in stillness. In quietness and rest you hear My voice.

It is difficult for you to come away from the cares and busyness of the world at times. As you draw aside, I will meet you and teach you many things. I will speak to you of things to come. Do not be concerned if this sounds strange. I will not let you be deceived or led astray. Seek Me as you are now, and test the spirits! My sheep hear My voice and know it.[39] Even now you are discerning more quickly when the enemy tries to deceive you.

I do not speak condemnation on you or on others. My voice is one of love and forgiveness. My love is great for My children. My gifts are free to all who will receive them.

Picture them as unread books on a shelf gathering dust and cobwebs. They contain a wealth of knowledge and understanding, but unless they are picked up and read, they are useless. By faith you must take up My gifts and use them. When you operate in My power and under My leading, the gifts will be operational in you. You must use them by faith. Obedience is your job; the results are up to Me.

I am your Maker. Am I not able to heal and restore that which I have made? Am I not able to set the captives free, to heal and deliver the mind and the body?[40]

The blood washes away sin and guilt. It renews the mind of the ravages of sin and guilt. The blood of Jesus cleanses you of *all* sin and guilt. Do not receive guilt! It is not of Me.

I love you! You cannot do anything that would separate you from My love. Did I not die for you? My love is great toward you,

---

39 John 10:4
40 Isaiah 61:1

My child. Come to Me and rest in My love. Eat of My food and be strengthened.[41] Rest comes to the weary. Rest in My love and be strengthened. I will meet all of your needs and strengthen your arms for battle. You will be ready when trials come. Set your eyes on Me, for your help cometh from the Lord.[42]

I am the Lord, and besides Me there is no other.[43]

SEEK ME FIRST

Come into My presence with praise and thanksgiving in your heart, for this pleases Me greatly. I long for your praises, just as a mother longs to be appreciated for all the things she does for her children.

Will you not recognize the daily blessings that are upon you?

I have given you so much, yet you long for more. I will not let your needs go unmet. You are Mine, and I watch over you. Indeed, I guard you jealously. When you seek Me first, all these other things are loosed in the spiritual realm.

Keep your eyes on Me and trust Me. You cannot truly praise Me if you do not trust Me. Have I not said it, and will I not accomplish it? I desire to see all of your needs met, but you must trust Me.

Faith is the key that unlocks the doors of the universe. Faith brings hope and trust. I long for your trust and your love; with these come true worship and praise.

Let go of the past. Whatever mistakes you have made, I use them to accomplish My purpose in your life. You cannot change the past—let it go!

Don't be concerned for the future. It belongs to Me. Yours is a daily walk. Take each day as it comes and don't look at

---

41   Isaiah 55:2
42   Psalm 121:2, KJV
43   Isaiah 45:6, NKJV

tomorrow. There is much to be done today. Don't let anxiety about the past or the future drain you of energy needed for today. Your task may be great, or it may be small; but if your eyes are not on Me, you will miss it. Seek ye first My kingdom, and all these other things will follow.[44]

I will not leave you comfortless; I have sent you a Helper.[45] He will guide you into all truth.[46] Trust Him. Seek Him out. Listen and obey. You must trust My voice; the Holy Spirit is My voice. I have given you discernment to hear My voice. There are times you know and times you question. Your spirit must bear witness to My Word, then you will know! If you still doubt, do not move on it. Wait upon the Lord. Trust Me. Your hope is in Me, the Hope of Glory. *Selah*.

IN QUIETNESS AND REST (FOR V. C.)

In quietness and in rest you shall come to Me. I will lead you and guide you in the steps you shall go. I will feed you, clothe you, and take care of you; for you are My child and I love you. It matters not if you are perfect. No man is perfect while on this earth and in the fleshly body. You are Mine, and I have not called you to be perfect. I have called you to have fellowship with Me. I long for you to share your innermost needs with Me.

I understand your feelings and your desires. I created you with the ability to have these feelings and desires. Do not condemn yourself, for I do not condemn you. I love you with an everlasting love.[47] My hand is upon you, and I watch over you. Indeed, I guard you jealously, for you are My child. I encamp My angels round about you. Do not fear, My child, for you will

---

44 Matthew 6:33
45 John 14:16, NKJV
46 John 16:13
47 Jeremiah 31:3

never be alone. I will always be with you. My hand is upon you, My daughter, and I am always here for you, always waiting with open arms.

I Make My Dwelling with You

I meet with you this morning at the appointed time. I make My dwelling with you, and I dine with you. I come to you in the night to comfort you and to guide you. In stillness and in rest, I come.

We will speak of many things: things past and things to come. Some things will be to share with others and some things will be for you alone.

I have called you for a work and a purpose. You question in the flesh, how can this be? But with Me all things are possible.[48] You have but to keep your eyes upon Me. I will lead you and direct you in the path that you should take.

I will guide you and counsel you with My hand upon you.

I keep you and guard you.

If you stray from My path, I will bring you back quickly. I guard you jealously, for I have seen your desire to serve Me. I have brought you to this place, My child, and you shall not go back into bondage. I have set you free that you might set others free.

I give to you the keys to My kingdom. The storehouse of My promises shall be opened up to you. My gifts will flow through you out to others. My anointing will be strong upon you to use you for My glory. Many forget that the glory is Mine and fall by the wayside. You must keep your eyes on Me, for I am your source. In everything you do, great and small, I am your source. I feed you and clothe you and give you strength for the day.

---

48 Matthew 19:26

I honor you, for you have honored Me and sought My will for your life. I am moving in your household, My child. Things seem to be in turmoil; I am stirring the waters to bring hidden things to the surface. I am shedding My light into every corner, and nothing shall remain hidden. I have promised to bring deliverance to your household, to set the captives free.[49]

Trust Me in this and keep your eyes on Me and not upon circumstances. Speak forth only good reports over your loved ones. Do not be amazed at the things you see, for have I not said it, and will I not do it?[50]

Think on these things, My child. *Selah.*

Bring Me Your Burdens

My child, I love you, and I long to hold you in My arms. As a mother hen broods over her chicks, so I brood over you.[51]

Do not be afraid to come. Run to Me and hide in Me. Bring Me your burdens and your heartaches. Bring Me your fears.

You do not have to feel spiritual to come. Come in humility and honesty. Pour out your heart to Me. Come to Me and lay your burdens down before Me; do not take them with you!

Am I not able to move on your behalf? Is anything too difficult for Me?[52] Do I not care for your loved ones and their needs, even as you do? I am able to save, even to the uttermost parts of the earth. I am able to save your loved ones. I am able to bring your children back. I am able to heal relationships. I am able!

Oh, My child, trust in Me and do not look at circumstances. They are nothing to Me, for I create circumstances. Praise Me in all things, knowing that I am in control, even of your life,

---

49 Isaiah 61:1
50 Numbers 23:19
51 See Luke 13:34
52 Jeremiah 32:27, NAS

for you have given it to Me. I accomplish that which concerns you—I, and not you![53]

Do not be concerned with your progress. Do not measure yourself by others or by their standards. I do not condemn you, neither am I disappointed in you. I love you, and I am pleased with your willingness to let Me change you. I am pleased with your progress. Do not receive condemnation from yourself or from your enemy!

Continue to submit yourself to Me, and I will do the rest. Go, and My love goes with you.

---

53   Psalm 138:8, NAS

four
BOUGHT WITH A PRICE

COME BOLDLY

> Which we have seen with our eyes…what we have looked upon, and our hands have handled, concerning the Word of life.
>
> —1 John 1:1, nkjv

You have beheld Me in many ways: the trees, the flowers that bloom, the birds that sing, the very air that you breathe. I am in all that exists, and you are in Me. You have come to Me freely, and I give to you freely. So come boldly, as a child comes to his parent, and know that I care about your smallest needs. I care about you! You are Mine; you are bought with a price. Therefore, glorify your Father who is in heaven.

WILL YOU NOT CARE?

> How lovely on the mountains are the feet of those who bring good news.
>
> —Isaiah 52:7

My child, you are Mine, and you are bought with a price! All that I have, I have freely given to you. All that I ask is that you share it with others. My Son died for all. Will you not tell them? Will you not share the good news with them?

Are they not important, even as you are important? I love you; I also love them, even the unlovable. The more unlovable they are, the more I love them!

Help them to break the chains that bind them. Will you not care?

UNCONDITIONAL TRUST

My daughter, you are mine; you are bought with a price.[54] Great was that price that was paid for you.

Great is your reward for your obedience to Me and to My Word.

My Word is true. It is living, for I am living. I perform My Word. Yes, I watch over My Word to perform it.[55] Look to Me, My child, and cling to the word that I have given you. Do you not trust Me? You cannot see the whole picture. You do not know what I am doing, but you must trust Me. I am a merciful God. Believe in Me. Look to Me for all your answers. The doctors do not have them.

I am the Way, the Truth, and the Life.[56] All things are in My power, and Mine alone. Trust in Me. I only want that which is best for all My children. This goes beyond physical comfort.

It is not always easy to grow, but grow you must if you are to accomplish the tasks that I have for you. I am your strength and your help in time of trouble. Keep your eyes on Me and do not look at circumstances. They are meaningless. I create circumstances! Therefore look to Me, hope in Me, and trust in Me, for I am your help: a very present help in times of trouble.[57] I speak peace to your mind and to your spirit. Peace in the midst of the storm. In quietness and in rest, come to Me. Lean

---

54 1 Corinthians 6:19–20
55 Jeremiah 1:12, NAS
56 John 14:6
57 Psalm 46:1, NKJV

on Me for support, and I will bring you through this. Again I say, trust Me! You are Mine; I watch over you. Never fear what I have for you. I am a good God, and I love you greatly with an everlasting love. My peace I give to you, even now. Receive it, My child, and rest in Me.

Overcoming

You are bought with a price, and you are Mine. Glorify Me in all that you do. Take no glory for yourself.

Have you ever made the lame to walk? You shall, My child, if you submit your will to Mine and your spirit to My Spirit. It is not easy, but I will teach you.

I love you, and I will not let you go, for I am a jealous God.

Come to Me when you are weary, and I will refresh you. Look to Me when you fall. I am always there.

I do not condemn you, for I remember that you are but flesh. It is My Spirit in you that enables you to overcome, and you *are* an overcomer. I have spoken it, and I will accomplish it. Look how far you have come. Yes, you still have weaknesses, but you are learning from them. I am teaching you spiritual truths through them, and you will overcome. Trust Me and submit your will to Mine. Look at Me and not at circumstances, for I am your circumstance!

I fulfill My Word; I watch over My Word to perform it.[58]

I am with you always, but I will not interfere with your will. You must submit daily, for the enemy will try to come in like a flood, but remember: the waters will not overflow you.[59] Look at Me, trust in Me, and I will deliver you. I can bring good out of every circumstance.

So go, My child, and take Me with you. Yes I go, but you must submit and listen to hear My voice.

---

58   Jeremiah 1:12, NAS
59   Isaiah 43:2, NAS

Be Faithful

Hear Me and obey! Come to Me when I call you, and do not wait. The need may be urgent. I have called you to pray for others, but most importantly, for your loved ones.

Be faithful in the small things, and I will call you to greater things, make you ruler of many things.[60] You are Mine; I have called you by name.[61] I watch over you jealously, for I am a jealous God. Put Me first in your life, and everything else will fall into its proper place.

You worry about your spouse and your children, but they are not yours. They are Mine. I will accomplish that which concerns them.[62] You are to pray for them. Pray My Word over them, and I will bring it to pass. I watch over My Word to perform it.[63]

I am also jealous over My Word. It is truth. It is life and health to all who receive it, for that is My promise.

I call to you, My child. Hear My voice and obey.

Be faithful in you prayers for you loved ones. You have been lax in you prayers for your family. They are in great need of them.

Remember: I watch over My Word to perform it. Trust Me to bring it to pass. Am I a man, that I should lie?[64] I think not!

I remember, however, that you are but flesh. I do not judge you if you miss Me. Do not receive condemnation.

I have made every provision for you. It is in My Word. Meditate on My Word. Pray over My Word. Stand firm in the Word, and I will bring it to pass.

Never fear, My child. I will not let you slip out of My hands. I have bought you with too great a price to let you go. You are

---

60   Matthew 25:23
61   Isaiah 43:1
62   Psalm 138:8, NAS
63   Jeremiah 1:12, NAS
64   Numbers 23:19

Mine. Rest in that promise. Rest in Me, for I watch over (guard) you jealously.

My love for you is great. You must believe that I love you. Remember the price that I paid for you, and rest in My love.

Look to Me

Lord, I'm not worthy to come to You and to ask Your forgiveness again!

Yes, you are worthy, My child, for I have made you worthy. I have bought you with a price, and the enemy cannot take that from you. I understand what you are going through. I see your heart and your desire to please Me in spite of the flesh. Your flesh will always hinder you. This is why you must keep your mind on Me.

Meditate on My Word, hide it in your heart, that you might not sin against Me.[65]

Feast on My riches. I have many gifts for you, My child. Look to Me, trust in Me, and I will bring it to pass—I, not you.

Trust Me and lean not on your own understanding.[66] Praise Me in all things. I know what is best for you, My child, and I will never bring you unhappiness. Your unhappiness comes from lack of trust in Me. Am I not God? Cannot I accomplish what I will? I spoke all things into existence. I move mountains, and I change circumstances. You are not to dwell on how I will change them, but you are to trust in Me and know that it is I who change them. You must stay out of My way and not hinder Me. I need your trust and your obedience.

---

65 Psalm 119:11
66 Proverbs 3:5

Guard Your Thoughts

Seek Me and I shall be found. Listen and you shall hear, for I am here waiting for you.

You are precious in My sight. Your heart has been found pure before Me. Yes, your struggles have been many, but your desire has been to do what is right.

I will teach you victory in Me and in My Word. I will make you strong, for indeed, My strength is perfected in your weakness.[67] You must lean on Me and rely on My strength, for your own strength will fail you. Guard your thoughts, take authority over them, and do not let them rule over you. Victory is in the mind.

You are Mine. You have been bought with a price. I will not let you go. I guard you jealously. The enemy seeks to destroy you, but he will not! I have put My hedge of protection around you. If you stumble, you shall not fall, for I have given My angels charge concerning you and your household.[68]

Seek Me early in the day, so you shall not miss what I have for you. I will order your steps aright before Me. My love is upon you, and I have many gifts for you. In due time you will receive them, when you are ready.

I am perfecting you. Do not be discouraged when you do not see things happening. I am in control, regardless of how things appear. I have heard your prayers for your children and your loved ones. I am working in their lives also. Continue to trust and believe for them. They are Mine, for I have called them by name! Not one will be left out. Stand back and watch the glory of the Lord!

It is I and not man who changes circumstances. Do not be amazed when these things come to pass. Know that I am God,

---

[67] 2 Corinthians 12:9, NAS
[68] Psalm 91:11, NKJV

who accomplishes all things concerning you and them. Keep your eyes on Me and not on circumstances, for your hope and trust is in Me. I alone will not fail you. When man fails you, I will not. I am here for you always, waiting.

five
CALLED OUT OF DARKNESS

WALK IN FREEDOM

Shake off your dust; rise up, sit enthroned, O Jerusalem. Free yourself from the chains on your neck, O captive Daughter of Zion.
—Isaiah 52:2

I HAVE SET YOU free, My daughter. The chains have been broken, yet you are still carrying the weight of them with you. They are entangled in your emotions (thoughts and feelings), your mind, and your will. These are a part of your flesh nature, which is at war with your spirit man.

When you feed your flesh nature it becomes stronger. The same is true of your spirit man. This is the reason fasting works; it denies the flesh its food. Your thoughts feed your flesh also. You must line up your thoughts with My Word. Use the Word to come against these thoughts.

Shake yourself free and rise up, My daughter! Lay aside the thoughts and fears that so easily entangle you. Go forth with shouts of victory and praise. I desire your praises, but they are also for you. They build you up in your inner spirit and bring you into communion and fellowship with Me. When you are walking in My presence, the flesh cannot rule in you.

Where there is light, there is no darkness. Which will you walk in? Which will rule over you? Which will you feed? One must become stronger, and the other become weaker. Balance does not work here, for the flesh battles the spirit and wants no part of him. You must feed your spirit more and deny the flesh. I am here to help you. Seek My presence and rest in My love. Do not receive condemnation, which is of the flesh. Receive My love! I am here for you always, to love you and to pick you up when you fall. Persevere in My love and walk in My freedom.

KNOW MY WORD

My child, you are Mine. I have called you by your name. I have redeemed you with My blood.

It matters not if you miss Me or fail to hear my voice; I will take care of it. I will also take care of you. I will grow you and nourish you. I will feed you with My Word.

My Word is your strength, and My joy is your strength!

Rest in My love and know that I will accomplish that which concerns you.[69] You cannot force your own growth, but you can help by getting proper nourishment. Seek My Word, read and meditate on My Word, and I will show you many truths. I fulfill My Word in you and in others. It matters not if you are able to see what I am doing. Stand firm on My Word and trust Me.

I will cause rivers of living water to flow forth from you.[70] You will nourish and strengthen others when they become weak from the battle. You will uphold their arms when they are tired. You will strengthen them with the water of My Word.

I am truth; I am light. In Me there is no darkness. You will overcome the darkness, as My light shines forth from you. Darkness cannot hide from Me. My light shines into every corner.

There is no shadow of turning with Me.[71]

---

69   Psalm 138:8, NAS
70   John 7:38
71   James 1:17, NKJV

I am your strength, your sword, and your shield. I gird you with truth. My Word is truth. Know My Word. Meditate on My Word. Stand on My Word.

The rest is up to Me. I love you, My child. Go forth, and I go with you!

Trust Is Peace

My hand is greatly upon you, My child. Seek Me and learn from Me. Know the truth, and the truth will set you free.[72] My Word is truth; it is light in time of darkness. My Word is truth; it is light to your whole body. Even your soul needs light, for darkness has tried to overshadow it and you.

Come to Me, for I am light. There is *no* darkness in Me. Rest in Me and trust in Me and I will bring all things to pass—I, not you. Do not hinder My work by getting in the way. Trust Me! In trust and faith comes total peace. I desire your happiness in all areas of your life. Can you trust Me to accomplish this circumstance for you? Trust is peace. Doubt is worry and fretting over things not seen.

I see things that are not as though they were![73] It is already accomplished in the heavenly realm. I accomplish all things pertaining to you. What I have ordained will come to pass. You help Me by trusting in Me and letting Me do the rest. Some things I will tell you and some things you must accept on faith. Your husband and children belong to Me. They are Mine, and I will accomplish all things pertaining to them.

Where is your faith? There is your peace also.

---

72 John 8:32
73 Romans 4:17

I Will Be There

> Be joyful always; pray continually: give thanks in all circumstances, for this is God's will for you in Christ Jesus.
> —1 Thessalonians 5:16–18

Praise Me, My child, and do not receive any fear, for I am not a God of fear but of love.

I only allow those circumstances in your life (and in your children's lives) that I can use to teach you new truths. Learn from them, and you will not have to go through them again. I am with you in every situation. My hand is upon you, even when it seems like total darkness around you.

My hand is upon your daughter also, and I will see her through this situation. She is walking in darkness and cannot see her way out. But I have not left her and will not leave her. I will guide her into the light. I will not allow her to slip away into the darkness. She is hurting and seeking relief from the hurt. I am the Balm of Gilead that soothes all hurts. I will be there for her, but she is not ready to reach out to Me yet. Man will fail to meet her needs. I am the friend that sticks closer than a brother![74] I will be there when all others have forsaken her. I love her unconditionally; you must love her unconditionally also. Only then will she turn to you for guidance and counsel.

Trust Me and allow Me to work in this. I walk with her and protect her in the darkness. I watch over My Word to perform it.[75] Speak words of faith over her. Pray for wisdom and guidance in how to relate to her. Believe for her, for she is unable to believe for herself right now. Stand in the gap for her; lift up

---

74 Proverbs 18:24
75 Jeremiah 1:12, NAS

her arms as Aaron and Hur did with Moses, for they are tired from the battle.[76]

And most of all, know that I love her even more than you do, so trust Me and praise Me in all circumstances.

Do Not Despair

> I am the LORD, the God of all mankind. Is anything too hard for me?
>
> —JEREMIAH 32:26

I am the great I AM, Creator of the universe and all that it contains. Every atom and every molecule came together at My command. Can I not take care of all your needs? Indeed, they are small compared to Creation. I spoke, and night became day. Even though they are small by comparison, your needs are not lost before Me.

I see your needs and your deep despair. You grieve for your children, who seem to have lost their way. They are My children also, and their needs are ever before Me. I will heal them and restore them to My fold, for I am their God. They have not forgotten Me. They have been deceived into seeking their own way. They have not learned yet to walk in total faith. You still struggle in this also, but I am with you always! I pick you up when you fall. I wait for you to call on Me so that I can answer you. I see your needs even before you ask. I see your hurts and your children's hurts. They are My hurts also. Give them to Me so that I can lighten your burden.

You cannot carry it on your own. It is too heavy, and you will fall. Trust Me to accomplish My Word and My promises.

Use praise to combat the darkness when it overtakes you. Praise will lift you above the circumstances and help you to see My hand at work. I love you, My child. Your struggles have been

---

[76] Exodus 17:8–13

great, but I see your desire for a pure heart. This is a precious and rare commodity in these times. Do not give up hope; do not despair, for I have called you by name and you are Mine!

I walk through the valley with you, and the darkness will not overpower you. Take My hand, and I will lead you into the light. I will lead your children also, for they are My children, even as you are My child. You need not fear for them. My love is upon them, and I guard them jealously. I will accomplish that which concerns them!

Know Your Source

I am the Lord thy God, Jehovah Rophe—the God who heals.

Bring Me your wounded spirit, with all its hurts from the past. I am Jehovah; I am Yahweh, and the One who heals. I heal all your hurts today, My child, for you have walked in darkness long enough. I set you free, My child. Do not go back into bondage! Do not receive the hurts from the past when they rise up, and do not dwell on them! Dismiss them as a part of the past that no longer exists. Look to the future and take each day as it comes, for each day has enough cares of its own.[77] Look to Me for answers and not to others. I am you source of strength and of victory. I alone keep you from falling, but you must lean on Me and look to Me, for I am your source.

I am a very present help in time of trouble.[78] I encamp angels round about you. I guide you and protect you, even when you don't know you are in danger. I feed you and clothe you. I strengthen you in your inner man.[79] I am your light in the darkness. Keep your eyes on Me, and the darkness will not overtake you.

---

77 Matthew 6:34
78 Psalm 46:1, NKJV
79 Ephesians 3:16, NKJV

Is it not light that causes darkness to flee, and not the other way around? I am the source of light, and that source is within you. The darkness must flee at your command. Know your source of strength, My child, and do not be deceived by the enemy! You can dispel the darkness when it tries to overtake you. You are mine, and I watch over you; but some things I leave for you to do.

Stand your ground and do not give place to the enemy.[80] He is powerless against you.

Casting Your Care

Come unto Me, and I will give you rest. You are weary from the battle, and it has been a great battle for you, My child. It has been a battle for your mind. The enemy has desired your mind, but he will not have it!

I have seen your tears, and I have heard your cries. Your desire is to please Me and do what is right in My sight, even though you long for earthly pleasures. Man may meet your needs of the flesh and your emotional needs, but only I can meet your spiritual needs! When you are lonely in spirit, this can be interpreted as physical loneliness.

Do not neglect your spiritual needs. I am always here waiting and longing to fill that spiritual void. Come and fellowship with Me, and I will feed you spiritual food so that you can be strong in your innermost spirit. My presence will comfort you, lead you, and guide you. You will not suffer loneliness in My presence. Learn to walk in My presence and commune with Me, even when going about your daily tasks. Your heart will sing for joy and be lifted up above every circumstance. Your feet will be light in their steps and not heavy. Difficult tasks will become easy.

---

80 Ephesians 4:17, NKJV

Cast all your cares upon Me, for I care for you. Give Me all your burdens and, indeed, your steps will be light! I care about your smallest needs, so do not delay to bring every care, great and small, to lay at My feet. Go, My child, with lighter steps. I go with you.

By Faith

I am here, My daughter, even as I have promised. I will always be here for you.

I have set My seal upon you—the seal of My Holy Spirit, who dwells within you. He keeps you in the midst of the battles and storms. Even when you are weak, He is strong and stays the hand of your enemy. I keep you, but I also strengthen you so that you will stand up and declare victory over the enemy. You are victorious, My child! I have made you victorious through My Son, Jesus. He fought the battle for you and He won.

He has taken the keys of the kingdom, and He has given them to you. You are to use them by faith. By faith you enter into My presence. By faith you are My child. Take up My gifts and My calling by faith, and I will order your steps aright and light your path for you. Do not doubt these things, for they shall come to pass. I have seen your heart and your desire to serve Me. You must put everything on the altar before Me, every possession and every relationship. You must trust Me in every area of your life. Do not just relinquish your will, but trust Me!

Submission without trust brings no joy. Perfect love cast out fear.[81] Know that My love is perfect toward you! Total trust will bring forth obedience in you. You must know that I will not mislead you or allow you to be misled, for I have seen your heart; you do not seek self-glory or fame.

---

81 1 John 4:18

You are content to be a tool, an instrument for My Holy Spirit to work through. For this reason I have called you My daughter and I have set My love upon you. You will share My love with others, yes, with many, and I will be with you and teach you what you should say.

For I am your sword and your shield, and I do battle for you. I will cause you to have peace, and, yes, even joy in the midst of the storm. In the eye of the storm there is calm and sunlight. I will be the eye of your storms! I will be your light when darkness falls, and it will not overtake you or come near you. Set your eyes upon Me, for I am your source. I go with you today, My daughter, and I keep you in My hand.

High Places and Deep Valleys

I am here, My child. I have called you to this appointed place. I have come that you might have abundant life.

Yes, your life is abundant. You have been blessed with many things that much of the world does not have. When you become depressed or burdened you are unable to see these blessings. You tend to think, where is my abundant life? But I never leave you, and I see you through these times. Yea, I even help you to focus your eyes back on Me, for truly, I am your source. I am the source for all your needs, both physically and spiritually. I am the light at the end of the dark tunnel. I will lead you out of the darkness into My marvelous light.[82]

Your enemy has battled long and hard to rob you of your peace and joy. Through this you have learned to lean on Me for strength and look to Me when you have no strength left. It has seemed like a hopeless, never-ending struggle, but I have taught you much. Can you praise Me for the darkness?

---

82 1 Peter 2:9, NKJV

Do you not know? Have you not heard? It is I who accomplish all things in you and for you.

Those who are blind must learn to operate in darkness. Indeed, they even use it to sharpen their other senses to focus in on things. I am sharpening your senses in the spiritual realm. I am fine-tuning your ear to hear My voice. I am teaching you to sense needs in others, that you might pray for or minister to them.

Sometimes you feel so alone, but you are not alone! I am with you, and I will never leave you or forsake you. My strong and powerful right arm is over you to protect you. The battle is not yours, but God's![83]

Praise Me in the midst of the storm. Praise Me in the high places and in the deep valleys.

I lead you through with My hand in yours. I guide your steps to keep you from stumbling in the darkness. I bring you to the other side and set you high upon a rock; your head will be high above your enemies. Yes, you will reach the other side, My child, and your joy will be complete, for thus saith the Lord: My Word is truth.[84]

---

[83] 2 Chronicles 20:15
[84] John 17:17

six
TRUST AND OBEY

LEARNING TO TRUST

My child, I am with you always, even to the ends of the earth. There is no place you can go that I will not follow and be with you. You are My chosen vessel, a vessel of honor, and I will give you honor wherever you go. My hand is upon you, and I will use you mightily.

I am training and preparing you even now. These lapses into the past will cease. You will soon gain control over the flesh, and it will rule over you no longer. You are learning to trust Me as that little child longed to trust her daddy and to be able to sit on his lap and be loved. As you learn to trust Me more, I will fill the void that was left unfilled as a child. No longer will you feel unloved or unworthy, for My love knows no boundaries.

I keep you, My child, when you are weak and cannot do battle for yourself. I put fences around you to keep you from straying too far, but My heart is heavy that you do not yet trust Me enough to bring all your troubles to Me. You have had many hurts and many rejections when you reached out for love, even as a child.

Soon you will minister to others who are hurt and rejected, for I have called and you have answered. Continue to come My child, for My arms are always open. You will not be rejected or ridiculed as in past times.

Lord, I want to bask in Your love today. Just let me feel Your love around me throughout the day!

Joy Comes Through Obedience

> We write this to make our joy complete.
> —1 John 1:4

These words were written in obedience to the Father, through the Holy Spirit. Joy comes through obedience. As you practice obedience, you are yielding to My Spirit. The more you yield to Me, the less control your flesh has. Trust and faith in Me transcends all obstacles. It frees Me to do My work in you and in others. Do not doubt, because you do not understand what I am doing. You cannot understand, for your understanding is limited by your fleshly body. You will understand when you are free from that body, but for now you must simply trust Me. Did I not say that My ways are not your ways?[85]

I have called you to trust and to obey. Then you will be free from worry and fear, and your joy will be complete in Me. Continue to seek Me. Continue in My Word and I will feed you My spiritual food. You will not go away hungry, for those that seek Me with all their heart will find Me.[86]

Tilling the Ground

> This is the message we have heard from him and declare to you: God is light; in Him there is no darkness at all.
> —1 John 1:5

---

85 Isaiah 55:8
86 Jeremiah 29:13

My child, I am the light of this earth. Those that are without Me walk in total darkness.

They hear without hearing and they see without seeing. They search in all the wrong places and do not look at the obvious. My love is great for them, and I long to bring them into the fold. You must pray for them, that the eyes of their heart be enlightened so that they may see and know the truth.[87] Bind every spirit of confusion and doubt, and loose the convicting power of My Holy Spirit to minister to them.

Prayer is so very important in reaching the lost. It is the forerunner to witnessing, for the heart must be ready to receive. Otherwise, the words fall on deaf ears and are lost. The heart must be tilled and fertile for the planted seed to spring forth. Pray for the watering of the Word, and bind every lying spirit that would steal the planted seed (the Word). Then you will see the harvest come forth in greater abundance!

Harvest takes much preparation before you go into the field to pluck the grain. When the harvest comes, remember: those that planted and watered have as great a part as the one who reaps. Your part is so very important.

You need not be fine of speech or flowery in words to win hearts for Jesus. Just speak what I put in your heart, and if I do not give you words to say, continue in your prayer for them. The time will come when the heart is ready to receive the word brought forth. The word may come from you or from someone else. Even so, great is your reward, for you have been obedient to My calling in you.

Hear My voice; listen to Me; trust and obey!

---

[87] Ephesians 1:18.

Faith Is the Key

My child, I am not slack concerning the promise I have given you.[88] I will bring forth the job that I have for you. I am concerned for you and for your every need. I am preparing you for many things, and I am teaching you trust and obedience. You must trust Me to fulfill My promises, even when you don't see any results. I am working on a different plane that you are on, and your sight is limited in what I am doing.

You must walk by faith. It is the forerunner of things to come. It is the key to My kingdom of riches and promises that I have poured out for you. I am not slack concerning My promises. Behold, I speak, and it comes to pass.

Faith comes from hearing and hearing from the Word of God.[89] My Word is in you. Meditate on My Word night and day. Line up your thoughts with My Word. Act on My Word when I speak to you. Trust Me to bring it to pass.

I am training you for difficult times. In the past you have run to and fro in these times. You must be prepared to look up for your help. Your help comes from Me and only from Me.

Trust Me. Build your faith in My Word. Read, meditate, learn from Me. Store it in your heart, and you will be ready for anything that comes. I am your God. I train your arms for battle. Take up your shield of faith and trust in Me.

You are an overcomer, for I have made you an overcomer. Your strength is in Me as you feast on My Word.

It will strengthen you and uphold you. It will remind you of all of My promises that will not fail. They will never fail, for I am Elohim, and I bring all things to pass that I have spoken. My Word is true, and I do not lie. I long for your trust. You

---

88 2 Peter 3:9, NKJV
89 Romans 10:17, NKJV

have trust in earthly things: parents and friends. Will you not trust in Me? I am your Maker and I desire only good for you.

Share My Love

Will you go into all the world and share My gospel? Will you not speak to those I put in your path today?

I have loved you, My daughter; I love them also. They need to hear this today. Share My love with them. It is so easy; it is not difficult, as you have thought. Just share what is in your heart. My love for you is great. It transcends all your transgressions. It is not limited by what you do. It is not conditional. I paid the price for it all through My Son, Jesus. He died for your sins, but not for yours only. It was also for the sins of the world. Some are ready today to hear and to respond. Are you ready? Just listen for My voice and be obedient to that which I have called for. I have been preparing you to hear My voice even when you are preoccupied.

When you hear My voice call, do not turn aside. Just act on My word, trust and obey.

I will be with you. It is not you but I who speaks to the heart. You are but My instrument!

Cultivate Faith

> My heart says of you, "Seek His face!" Your face, Lord, I will seek.
> —Psalm 27:8

Seek Me early and you shall find Me.[90] Call unto Me and I shall answer you and show you great and mighty things.[91]

---
90 Proverbs 8:17, kjv
91 Jeremiah 33:3, nkjv

I call to you in many ways throughout the day. You must be alert to be aware of My voice. Train your ear to hear. Listen for My voice. Come to Me often and seek My face. I will help you to learn these things. I will teach you discernment, that you will be able to judge what you hear. You are My child; I will not lead you astray. You must be willing to follow My voice, and practice obedience and discipline.

I long to teach you many things, My child, but you are not ready. I am tilling the soil and making it ready. That which I plant will spring up quickly once the ground—your heart—is fertile and ready. This requires much trust from you. You must trust Me in all things and lean not to your own understanding.[92] Trust overcomes fear, then joy springs forth. The joy that you have been looking for and hoping for comes by trusting Me.

I would not harm you or your loved ones. I only allow that in your life which will cause you to grow. It takes adversity sometimes to get your attention (and your loved one's attention).

Seek Me early in the day. Listen for My voice constantly, and many trials can be averted. Cultivate faith and trust in My Word and in My voice.

I am with you always.

Kindle Afresh the Gift

> Kindle afresh the gift that is in you through the laying on of my hands.
> —2 Timothy 1:6, NAS

> For God has not given us a spirit of fear.
> —1 Timothy 4:14, NKJV

You are Mine; I have called you. Come away from the world and seek Me. I will show you great and mighty things. You are

---
92 Proverbs 3:5

Trust and Obey

Mine; I have redeemed you. I go before you, and I show you the way. Go forth and speak that which I have given you.

You are My child, and I will not lead you astray. Neither will I leave you, nor forsake you.[93]

Your loved one belongs to me, and the results of your obedience belong to Me. You are but to act and speak forth what I give you.

The mountain is not a mountain to Me. I am God; I created mountains. I spoke them into existence. I speak to you today, My child, and tell you to come against this mountain. It must bow down before Me. Speak My Word and watch; will I not perform it? Act on My Word and leave the results to Me. You need not beg or plead. Simply speak My Word.

I watch over My Word to perform it, and I watch over you.[94] Your loved one is in My hands. She trusts Me. Will you not trust Me also?

Do not doubt My Word. Have I told you anything that does not line up with My written Word? Act quickly and do not delay. Timing is important in obedience. Follow through when I tell you to act. I am an orderly God; I do not offend. If I tell you to do something, then do it. You are My instrument. It is My power flowing through you that brings results.

I am the resurrection and the power. I bring life to all. Your life is in My hands. All life is Mine. Death is but a stepping stone into My world and eternal life. I call when I call; do not fear. Your love and obedience are precious to Me. I love you with an everlasting love. You are Mine, redeemed by the blood of My Son, Jesus Christ. His blood sets My people free from sin, sickness, and death.

---

93 Hebrews 13:5
94 Jeremiah 1:12, NAS

You are free; go set others free. Go, My child, and I am with you. Love as you go. Show love, mercy, and grace to others, even as I show to you. *Selah.*

I am with you.

Faith Is the Victory

> The Lord is your keeper; The Lord is your shade on your right hand.
> —Psalm 121:5, nas

My child, I have kept you, watched over you, and protected you, even in your rebellion and sin. How can you doubt My love for you? I am strengthening you each day, even though you do not know it yet.

Trust Me and draw near to Me, and I will teach you all that you need to know. I am your keeper. I watch over you and protect you. I guard you jealously.

I would that you put Me first in your life, above all else. Your job, your family, your friends—every relationship—must be submitted to Me. Remember: "Unless the Lord builds the house, They labor in vain who build it."[95]

This is true of every relationship, every area of your life. You must loose them to Me before I can give them back to you. If you want to see Me work, let go!

Truly, what you bind on Earth is bound in heaven.[96] Stop holding your loved ones in bondage. Loose them to Me so that I can work, then stand back and watch My handiwork. You truly will see great and might things you have not known.[97]

I love you and I desire your happiness and peace of mind. This comes through Me and not others. This comes through trusting

---

95 Psalm 127:1, nas
96 Matthew 16:19
97 Jeremiah 33:3, nkjv

in Me and in My Word. I watch over My Word to perform it.[98] My Word is truth.[99] Stand on My Word and proclaim it for your loved ones, but don't take them back up. Don't worry or fret about them.

Total peace of mind in every circumstance is a result of total trust in Me. Begin by praising Me!

My presence enables you to loose your faith, which comes from the Holy Spirit. My presence brings you peace and joy. Begin every day with praise. I desire your praises and your fellowship. Wait before Me. Sit at My feet and I will teach you many things.

My Word is truth. Know My Word! It is your weapon in warfare. When you know My Word, your faith is not easily shaken. You will not fear the battle, since you will know the outcome. The battle is already won. Faith is the victory. Your shield of faith is able to quench every fiery dart of the enemy.[100]

The Lord Is My Strength

Thy face I shall seek, Lord.

I am filled with joy that you have sought Me this morning, for you have been obedient to My calling. I have called, and you have answered.

I have heard your cries also—those heart-rending cries that tell Me how much you are hurting. It's OK, My child, to cry out. It is OK to be human. I do not expect you to be strong every moment. I am here to be strong on your behalf when you are weak and hurting. You have not failed because you are not perfect. I have already told you that you will never be perfect. Quit looking at your shortcomings and look at Me, the author

---

[98] Jeremiah 1:12, NAS
[99] John 17:17
[100] Ephesians 6:16

and finisher of your faith![101] I overcome for you; I lift up your arms and strengthen them for battle. You will not be overtaken. You shall not be moved, for I am your God who delivers you!

I set you free that you might go and set others free. I am working in you and through you to accomplish My will and My purpose. Your obedience is so very important! Do not doubt that you hear My voice, for you belong to Me and I guard you jealously. I will not allow you to be deceived. You will not follow a stranger's voice as long as you have your eyes on Me, so trust Me and trust My voice. If you truly have doubt, wait for confirmation. Then you shall surely know. I have called you, My child, and My hand is upon you to deliver you through these hard times.

You have been grieving lost relationships, and this is normal. I see you through and even shorten the process. Brighter days are coming and, indeed, will come quickly, if you keep your eyes on Me. It is I and not you that accomplish these things. I am your source of strength to make it through. I am the Lord that healeth thee—of all thy hurts, fears, anger, and hatred.[102] Even those buried deep shall be brought to the light for healing. You shall be free, My daughter!

LISTEN AND FOLLOW

I am here, My child. Listen to Me and follow My voice, for I will not lead you astray. As long as you seek Me and My will for your life, I will not allow you to be deceived.

I have called you to a work, and I am training you. Be ready to move in the night when I call. Be ready to hear My voice and to act on My Word. It may seem strange at times, but you must trust Me and act on My Word. I will not lead you astray and I will not offend others.

---

101 Hebrews 12:2
102 Exodus 15:26, KJV

Trust and Obey

I have called you to a walk of obedience and trust; herein lies the key that opens the door to all other works and gifts that I have for you. It is easier to trust than to obey, but the trust must come first for the obedience to be possible. I am with you, and I see your progress.

There will be rough days ahead. There will be storms and trials, but you must trust Me and keep your eyes on Me, for I am you source—I, and no other! No man can meet all your needs. I and only I can be with you at all times and know all of your needs. Indeed, I know your needs even before you ask, and before you call I have prepared the answer.

Your needs are no small thing to Me, even as the needs of your children are no small thing to you. I have seen and heard the cries of your heart for your children. I have seen, and behold, the answer is coming, even quickly, My child, for you have waited long. You have waited long and you have been faithful to believe for your children! I am coming to rescue them from the darkness. With My powerful right arm I defeat their foes, and I will lift them up onto a high place. Their heads will be above their enemies, and they will see clearly what I have done for them.

The time is short, and I must move quickly. Do not be alarmed at the things that take place to accomplish My purpose. Just look to Me and know that I AM, and that I accomplish My purpose in them, even as you have asked and believed.

Stand and see the glory of the Lord.

I accomplish My purpose in them and in you, My child, for you have asked Me and I have seen your heart. I am healing the hurts of the past, and you will have a heart full of love for your husband and your children. It will be a perfect love that does not judge or criticize. You will also love yourself as you have not been able to do in the past.

seven

POSSESS THE LAND

I Am Your Provider

I HAVE CALLED YOU, My child, to do battle for your family. Trust Me; set your face toward Me, and let praise be continually in your mouth, for I bring all things to pass.

Seek Me, rather than earthly riches. Do not be pressured in your job to provide for your family, for I am your provider. I meet all of your needs. You have but to trust Me and put Me first in your life, for I am a jealous God.

I am jealous over My Word also. I watch over My Word to perform it.[103]

You are anointed to My service, My child. I have called you, and I will prepare you. Do not look to man, but to Me. I train your hands to do battle, to take captive and possess the land that I have given you.

Feast at My table. Seek My presence and dwell in it. Cultivate faithfulness in the land. Plant the seeds of My Word in your heart and in others. I will water it and cause the increase. You have but to seek Me and obey Me. I am your provider, and I make every provision for you, provision for your spiritual growth and for your earthly needs.

---

103 Jeremiah 1:12, NAS

Ask and it shall be given you, seek and you shall find, for I am the door to abundant life and prosperity![104] Seek Me first, and everything else will fall into place. I am your place of abundance and prosperity. I provide for My children. I long to bring you into that abundance, but you must learn to seek Me first for all your needs and to enter into My rest. It is a walk of total faith in Me, for I meet your needs, not man. Men will fail you. I will never fail you.

Have I left you comfortless? Have I not given you My Holy Spirit to remind you of these things? He will lead you into all truth! Seek Him daily for guidance and counsel. Trust Him, for We are One.

Do Not Be Deceived

Come and dine, My child. Feast upon the riches of My Word. My Word is truth. It is living. It is sharp and active, even to the pulling down of strongholds.[105] There are no strongholds beside Me. They are nothing to Me.

I created every angelic being. I cast Satan and his angels out of heaven. Their activity is limited to this small space around Earth, and they stole power through bluffs and deception. Do not be deceived, My child. You are Mine, and your enemy has no power over you. Do not fear or give him any ground.

Even as I told Moses, I tell you: every place whereupon the soles of your feet shall tread shall be yours.[106] Possess the land for your husband and your children. Stand on My Word and believe for them. Make no negative statements that nibble away at your faith. Keep your eyes on Me and not on circumstances. Circumstances are nothing to Me. I change them in a moment's

---

104 Matthew 7:7
105 2 Corinthians 10:4, NKJV
106 Joshua 1:3

time. Trust Me to bring all things to pass concerning your family. Am I not God and not a man, that I should lie?[107]

Search My Word and know My truths, that you may believe, that your faith may be strong. I watch over My Word to perform it.[108] I perform My Word in you and through you, for you are My chosen servant, a vessel of honor, fit for My service.

My anointing is upon you, for I have called you. You have only to walk in that anointing. I will teach you how to walk, and you will lack no tool (spiritual gift) to accomplish the task that I will put before you. Now is the time to begin your faith walk. Search and study My Word and stand firm upon it, and I will bring it to pass. For I am God, and besides Me there is no other![109] Be ye holy, as I am holy.[110] This can only be accomplished through Me. Cease striving and know that I can bring it to pass.

Cease striving and rest in Me. I accomplish all things, not you.

The Sifting Process

I am pleased that you are seeking Me, child. I come to sup with you and fellowship with you. You are My child, and I long for your fellowship, just as you long for your children's fellowship. My love is great upon you, and I desire your praise and worship.

It pleases Me that you have trusted Me with your life—your family, circumstances, and job. I work all things together for good, for indeed I have called you by name.[111] Your family also belongs to Me, and I will also work their circumstances out

---

107 Numbers 23:19
108 Jeremiah 1:12, NAS
109 Isaiah 45:5, NKJV
110 1 Peter 1:16, KJV
111 Romans 8:28

for good. They will possess the land that I have called them to possess. I will surely lead them and guide them by the hand, even as I have guided you through your darkest hour. Even when you could not feel My presence, I never left your side.

I will see them through their dark hour also. I guard them jealously. The enemy cannot touch them to destroy them. He can only sift them like wheat. This sifting separates the chaff from the grain. It is a refining process. Only the grain is able to bear fruit. I am removing the chaff, the clutter in your lives, that is keeping you from bearing fruit.

Trust is the key! I work quickly when you trust Me, and it is less painful. Let go of your husband and your children and let Me do My work. I do not need your help! You do not have to be their conscience. Love them unconditionally where they are. This is the way I have loved you. They need your love and your reassurance that it is always there. Reach out to them and love them without condition!

Victory Can Be Yours

> I am the Lord, the God of all mankind. Is anything too hard for me?
> —Jeremiah 32:27

My child, I am teaching you many things. The confessions of your faith are very important. You must speak them forth in your prayers and in your conversation. Speak forth the promises that I have given you, not lest I forget, but lest you forget.

Faith is built through the spoken word, and not just the written Word. Confess My Word and My promises in your prayers and in your conversation. I watch over My Word to perform it.[112] The heavens and the Earth were created by My

---

112 Jeremiah 1:12, NAS

spoken word. My Word is powerful and living, sharper than any sword.[113]

This is your tool against your enemy. My Word and faith in My Word are your weapons. Use them often to strengthen your faith and to show yourself to be strong in the eyes of your enemy.

I came that you might have abundant life.[114] Do not be robbed. Call forth My Word and speak it into action! Then walk in faith, making no confessions against My Word. Your enemy must know that you believe what I say. Then he will know that he is defeated.

Victory can be yours, My child, through faith and trust in Me and in My Word. I watch over My Word to perform it.[115] I watch over you, for you belong to Me. Never forget this, My child, lest you be torn to pieces.

You must show yourself to be strong in the presence of your enemy.

A Growing Process

All things are possible to him who believes.
—Mark 9:23, nkjv

Yes, My child, all things are possible in the spirit realm. I am not limited by time or space. I see those things that are not as things that are.[116] Your faith must grow to the point that you also can see things that are not as though they are. This can only be done through Me, through My Spirit. It is a growing process, and you must start from where you are.

---

113   Hebrews 4:12
114   John 10:10, nkjv
115   Jeremiah 1:12, nas
116   Romans 4:17

Spiritual growth requires spiritual food. My words are life and health to body and spirit. They will nourish and strengthen you. Meditate on My words and My promises throughout the day. Seek new truths in My Word. Nothing is new, but they will be new to you.

Develop a faith walk and dwell only on positive thoughts. Negatives will tear down your faith. Build rather than destroy.

Praise Me in all things, knowing that I am in control. If I allow it, it is for a reason. The enemy can do nothing unless I allow it. Praise brings My presence into the situation and the enemy is rendered powerless.

Behold, all things are possible to him who believes.[117] Praise will keep your eyes on Me rather than on the situation. I am your strength to see you through each trial. Each trial becomes a small thing when I am used as the measuring stick. It is nothing to Me. I created the Earth and everything in it. I created the universe, the vast expanse of heavens that you cannot comprehend. Is a trial anything to Me?

I change circumstances in a moment's time, when not hindered by your fear and doubt. You must loose it to Me and let Me work it out in My way. Trust Me. When you praise Me, you are able to sense My presence. You will feel My love. Then it will be much easier to trust Me fully.

You are Mine. I delight in you and watch over you. I give to you the keys to My kingdom. Use them! Many treasures are stored up for you, waiting. Trust and faith are the keys. Cultivate them in My Word.

Stand in the Gap

I set My love upon you today, My child, for you have sought My face and My will for your life.

---

[117] Mark 9:23, NKJV

Yes, you have even resisted thoughts of temptation and taken authority over them. See how My Spirit fills the void? See how you are prepared to move in the spirit when the need arises? Your children need for you to stand in the gap for them and to take authority over the enemy for them. They are walking in darkness and do not know how to overcome, and what they have learned they have forgotten. But I will bring it back to their remembrance, and I will teach them.

Yes, I will teach them many things that they do not know, and they will walk with Me as children of the light. The darkness will not overtake them to destroy them, for My hand is over them and My protection is upon them. They are Mine, for I have called them by name and I will not let them go. Nothing in their lives happens by accident. Everything that I allow I use to draw them unto Myself.

As I have set you free, go set others free. My love is upon you, and I prepare you ahead of time for the needs as they arise. Even as you rose up to intercede for your daughter today, you will rise up to intercede for others. You will also minister to the needs of others as they arise.

Continue to seek Me daily and to set your heart toward Me like a flint. Do not be deterred or discouraged because of what you do not see. Faith is the substance of things hoped for and the evidence of things not seen.[118] I am not limited by time or space. Therefore, it is important for you to trust Me and walk by faith. Speak forth things that are not, by faith. Speak forth My Word, and I will honor it, for indeed, I watch over My Word to perform it.[119]

I watch over you too, My child. I will not let you slip away from My grasp. The enemy will not touch you to do harm to you. His threats are lies; do not receive them into your spirit,

---
118   Hebrews 11:1
119   Jeremiah 1:12, NAS

for they eat away your faith. Stand firm on My Word in all things, and I will bring it to pass.

Thank you for coming today, My child. These times are very precious to Me.

Faint Not and Hold Fast, a Word for Times of Warfare

My child, I have called you today, and you have answered. I hear your cries for help and your prayers in the night. I have heard your cries and your help draweth nigh![120]

I have created you to be an instrument of praise. I have ordained that praise come forth from your lips. I have seen your desire for true worship. You are learning to praise Me even in difficult times when your body is under physical attack.

I see your heart's desire for your children. I love them also, and I will not let them go. I seek them out to bring them back safely into the fold. You are right not to receive fear when you do not know where they are. I know, and My hand is upon them. I call them and they will hear My call. I watch over My Word to perform it in them and in you![121]

Faint not and hold fast to My promises, for they will come forth. I am preparing you for the coming battles. I will strengthen you and make your armor strong. Do not lie down and submit to these attacks. Even when they are physical, get up and refuse to succumb! Use praise and the Word for your weapons of warfare.

Warrior King

Yes, child, I am here. Read Psalm 18.

---

120 Luke 21:28, ASV
121 Jeremiah 1:12, NAS

Yes! Truly You are my strength, and Your right hand sustains me. Hallelujah!

I do for you what I did for David, My daughter, for you are My chosen one. I have sustained you and uplifted you in the midst of the battle. My hand is upon you, and I will not let you go. Yes, I do battle in the heavenlies for you, My daughter, even as I did for David. His enemies were strong, but they did not overtake him, for My hand was upon him and I would not let them overtake him. The battle is Mine.

You cannot change circumstances. You cannot even change yourself, but you can and must submit to Me. It is I who accomplish all things pertaining to you.

You have but to trust Me and to trust My Word. My Word will set you free, for My Word is truth.

When I call to you, you must come. Sometimes you feel as if you cannot hear Me, but you must not rely on feelings. I am training you to be able to hear My voice, no matter what. I am training you to hear quickly and to act quickly. You must come often to train your ear to hear My voice. This is of utmost importance at this time. I am able to do battle for your family; all you have to do is trust Me to take care of them. I love them with a greater love than your love, for My love is perfect and pure, lacking in nothing. My love is unconditional and does not condemn.

Do not be in bondage to a format in your prayer. You must be open to My leading and the quickening of My Spirit. I will lead you into all truth, all knowledge, for I am truth and knowledge.[122] It is Mine to give.

I am setting you free so that you can go set others free! This is your training ground. Hear My voice and come.

---

122 John 16:13

I love you, My child, and My hand is upon you. I see you through the battles. Soon, your head will rise up above the battle and you will walk through, untouched by the enemy. Rise up in your spirit man and do not be dismayed, for the battle is not yours but God's![123] Thus saith the Lord, your Savior!

Weapons of Warfare

My child, I am here this morning, as I am every morning. I have called you to this place of meeting. I have called you forth to be a router of your enemy.

Praise Me in all things, yes, but do not back down when faced with spiritual attacks. Praise Me also for the weapons I have given you and for the authority to use them.

Praise Me for the word I have given you, every promise written or spoken. These are your weapons of warfare. My Word is truth, whereas your enemy lies. He whispers lies and deceit in your ear to condemn you. Know My Word—the truth—and My Word will set you free.[124] Speak out My Word against your enemy. Confessing My Word brings it forth to fruition. My Word goes forth to accomplish My will and My purpose. It is strong, it is powerful, to the bringing down of strongholds![125]

This is My word to you this morning. Store it in your heart and use it, for I have called you and I have chosen you to do battle for your family in the heavenly places. This is where the battle lies. You shall not fear for their safety. I have put a hedge of protection around them. You shall call forth My Word to fruition over them. You shall call forth their spirit man to rise up and take authority over the flesh. Speak forth My Word and My promises over them, and make no negative confessions to

---

[123] 2 Chronicles 20:15
[124] John 8:32
[125] 2 Corinthians 10:4

defeat your faith. Do not give place to the enemy, but give place to My Word.[126]

Speak My Word over your life also. I am here for you always, and I honor My Word for you always. You are My child, called by My name. My hand is upon you to lead you and to guide you, even through the waters. They shall not overtake you. Indeed, I lift you up above the waters and set you in a dry place.

Go forth today, and I go with you. Listen for My voice as you go, for I go with you. Listen for My voice as you go, for I speak to you throughout the day.

---

126 Ephesians 4:27, NKJV

eight
YOU ARE MY WITNESS

Go Forth

The life was manifested, and we have seen, and bear witness, and declare to you that eternal life which was with the Father and was manifested to us.
—1 John 1:2, nkjv

I proclaim to you life eternal through My Son, Jesus Christ. You are My witness to the world. Go forth and proclaim that which I have given you. Proclaim and do not fear. You are My voice to share the good news of My Son.

Great is My pleasure in those who will share this news with others. How will they hear if you don't tell them? The need is great, My child, for those that would be attentive to My voice, hear Me, and obey.

Their life may be in your hands. What if you are the only one that can tell them or that will tell them? Will you not act and trust Me to do the rest?

Tools to Be My Witness

My child, I have called you and I have given you the tools to be My witness. You have all the tools My Son had through My Holy Spirit. You have but to use them. Obedience is the key. When you hear My voice, act on it.

There are times I would not have you to eat or to drink until you have sought Me. It is not that it is wrong to drink or to eat first, but you must learn to seek Me first, to hear My voice and act on it.

I do not condemn you when you miss Me. You have but to confess it, and I can use it to teach you. I long to teach you many things, but first you must get still before Me; wait on Me. Then you must learn to act on what I say. Even this I will teach you. Surely I will not forsake you, for I have called you forth as My servant to heal the sick, raise the dead, and make the blind to see. Every work that Jesus did, you will do. Did He not say, "Greater things shall you do because I go to the Father"?[127]

Am I a man, that I should lie?[128] All it takes is obedience and a listening ear. I am teaching you these things now. You are to act on My Word; the results are up to Me. Do not worry about the results; just act on My Word. Hear My voice and obey, for I have called you as My servant. A servant obeys without question, even when the command does not seem not logical. This takes faith, which comes from My Word. Know My Word. Study My Word. I will set you free and you will set others free.

Freely I have given, freely give.[129] My love is set on you and My hand is over you. You need not fear.

Remember Jeremiah 33:3. You cannot comprehend all that I will show you, but act on My Word and trust Me. Again I say, trust Me!

You Are My Instrument

My child, hear Me today and follow My voice. I have called and you have come. I am pleased with your obedience, My child. I know it was difficult for you to arise this early.

---

[127] John 14:12
[128] Numbers 23:19
[129] Matthew 10:8

I come when I come, and I call when I call. You must be ready to hear My voice and to obey, if I am to use you.

I have called you to be an instrument of My love. I have called you to have compassion on the weak and the downtrodden. I have set My love upon you so that you may love others. I have called you, My child, and I will accomplish that which concerns you.[130] You have wondered about the things that I have told you concerning the works you will do. Yes, these things will be accomplished. My hand is upon you.

It is I who perform miracles. You will be an instrument of My power. I am teaching you obedience and submission. You must be ready to move when I call. You must not be afraid of what man thinks of you. I am able to surround you with favor, even as I did with others (Solomon, David, Joseph, Daniel). I will call others to lay gifts at your feet, for you are My chosen one and I have seen your heart.

Your struggle has been great, My daughter. Indeed, you have felt dishonored in your own house at times, but you shall have honor, My chosen one. You shall be My servant, called by My name. I have redeemed you and I will keep you! My hand is upon you, and no one shall pluck you out of My hand.

Today is a day of new beginning. I have called you to journey with Me, and I will teach you many things.

I Can Use You!

Be still, My child, for I am here waiting. I am here at this appointed hour to meet with you. Yes, we shall speak of many things during these times. Today we will speak of you.

You are here and I am pleased, for I have called you. Many times it has been difficult for you to hear Me. Your mind has been clouded by oppression and feelings of unworthiness.

---

130 Psalm 138:8, NAS

Indeed, it has been hard for you to believe that I would meet with you and you alone. The things you have written have been written in faith, for you have not had a strong sense of My presence upon you. I would not have you operate on feelings and emotions, but on faith!

As you begin to move under My direction, the anointing will come. You must be obedient to My Word and not to feelings. Your obedience thus far pleases Me. As you learn to move in obedience, I will use you in a greater way. It matters not if you feel "spiritual" at that moment. I move when I move, and you are the instrument I have chosen. Your obedience is necessary to accomplish My will for that appointed time. Look not to self but to Me. It is My power and My Spirit flowing and operating through you. You are but an instrument. Indeed, I can use a donkey—and have—if no man will cooperate, to accomplish My purpose.[131] Do you think the donkey was worthy?

You will never be perfect. You have been made worthy through the blood of My Son, which was shed for you! Would you limit the cleansing power of that blood? Indeed, it is a continual cleansing and renewing process. Just submit to Me daily and trust Me to do the rest.

I can accomplish the changes in you that you so desire. You cannot, so quit trying and loose them to Me. Are they not My responsibility? Do I not honor My Word? My hand and My love are greatly upon you, My child. Go in peace, and I go with you.

Tempered Like Iron

Not by might, nor by power, but by My Spirit, saith the Lord.

—Zechariah 4:6, kjv

---

131 See Numbers 22

All things were created by Me and without Me nothing was created.[132] By My Spirit they were created as I spoke forth My Word. My Word is truth and does not return to Me void.[133] My Spirit moves according to and in line with My Word! Cling to My Word and My promises, and do not let them go. Hide them in your heart. Confess them with your mouth.

Train your ears to hear My Word and not negative words that will destroy your faith. Train your mouth to speak My Word and words of faith over every situation! Do not receive negative words or negative thoughts. They will only tear down your faith. Faith comes from hearing My Word and knowing My Word. You must also know your enemy and be aware of his schemes. He will try to tear down your faith through analytical thoughts.

I do not operate as man would, in the physical realm. I transcend the physical, and I use the foolish to confound the wise.[134]

I will use you, My daughter, to accomplish many things. I have chosen you as an instrument of My Holy Spirit. I will use you mightily, for you have submitted yourself to Me and to My direction for your life. You have clung to your faith, even in difficult times. You have believed My Word. My Word will set you free, and your household. You have believed for them, and I honor your faith. I will bring them back to the fold, for they are My sheep. They belong to Me, and I guard them jealously. I guard and watch over you also, and I will see you through every trial that comes your way.

You will be like the mighty oak, made stronger by each wind it withstands. You will be tempered like iron made stronger by the heat. You will not fear what man can do, for you will know

---

132 Colossians 1:16
133 Isaiah 55:11, NKJV
134 1 Corinthians 1:27

the strength and power of your God! I hold you in the palm of My hand—My strong and mighty right hand—and you will not fall, nor will you fail, for I am with you always, even to the ends of the earth.[135] *Selah.*

Redeemed for a Purpose

Yes, My child, it is difficult at times to hear My voice, especially when there are many thoughts going through your mind. It is difficult to be still before Me at times. This is your training ground. I am training your ear to hear, even in difficult situations. I will call upon you in the hour of need, whenever that hour may be. I would have you ready to hear My voice at all times.

I am here to reaffirm My call on your life and reaffirm the love I have for you, for I am your Father. I have begotten you, and I will not leave you or forsake you.[136] I have called you by name and you are Mine. I have redeemed you for a purpose: to love others, as I have loved you. Set others free, as I have set you free, and your freedom shall soon be complete, My child! No longer will you be beset by heaviness and weariness. Your trust is in Me, and I have seen and honored that trust. I have seen your struggles; I have heard your cries! I am the Lord who healeth thee![137]

I am your creator and your redeemer, and I have called you out of the darkness into My light.[138] Nothing shall be impossible to thee, for you are My child, called by My name![139] Did not Jesus say, "Greater works than these you shall do, because

---

135 Matthew 28:20
136 Hebrews 13:5
137 Exodus 15:26, KJV
138 1 Peter 2:9
139 Luke 1:37

I go to the Father"?[140] Do not wonder how this shall be. Just keep your eyes focused on Me. We will take one step at a time, and I will be with you each step of the way. You will not fall by the wayside, for I have already prepared you. Continue in your walk and come to Me when I call.

Come early, and I will order your day for you. It may not be what you have planned, but it will be what I have planned.

You Are an Heir

I see your heart, My daughter, and your desire to please Me. Yes, you have shortcomings in the flesh and are weak in some areas, but the desire is there at all times. I see your heart, and this is why I have chosen you. I will fill your heart with longing for My fellowship and My presence.

It is sitting in My presence that will make you strong, even in the areas where you are weak. It is My presence that gives you peace and joy in My Holy Spirit.

I wait for you, My child, to come to Me. I wait with open arms. I am here when you need Me. I am here always, even when you do not feel worthy. I have made you worthy, for I have clothed you with My righteousness.

You are an heir to all that is Mine. I have clothed you with majesty and grace. I watch over you and protect you. I set guards around you, for you have believed that I am with you. Your faith has not wavered that I am with you always, and I honor that faith.

Though a multitude come against you, you will not be harmed.

Do not be alarmed at these things or doubt that I will use you. I go before you and prepare the way, even as I prepare you. You will be ready on time. You shall not be early or late!

---

140   John 14:12

My child, do not doubt that these things shall come to pass. Do not doubt that I care about your smallest needs. I am working in every area of your life; you will be lacking in nothing.

You have tried to close off your feelings because you are afraid of temptation. Do not fear, for I am able to overcome temptation! Do not be afraid to feel love for others. Love and lust are not the same. You have always feared or questioned your feelings for others. I have given you a tender heart; it is nothing to fear.

You have also feared rejection if you reach out. Fear is not of Me. Some reject Me, but many receive Me. They must be given opportunity to receive. You must overcome fear and intimidation. I am here to help you.

Unfamiliar Ground

Hear Me, My daughter, for I have spoken. Hear Me well.

Do not be afraid of the things I have spoken. Fear is not from Me.[141]

I have called, and you have answered. But your heart fears the unknown. You fear to tread on unfamiliar ground, but I am with you to help you overcome this fear. Reach out to the new and unfamiliar as a chance to learn and grow. I am with you to help you. It can be a time of learning and excitement—even a time of joy!

Look to Me to lead you and guide you through. I will retrain your thought processes to look forward to new experiences rather than fear them. Go with joy and anticipation at what I have in store for you.

---

141   See 2 Timothy 1:7

To Contact the Author

nancyngore@aol.com